1000 LOVE AND SEX QUIZ

1000 LOVE AND SEX QUIZ

Dr. Anil Aggrawal

Rupa & Co.
CALCUTTA
ALLAHABAD BOMBAY DELHI

An Original Rupa Paperback
First Published 1992 by
Rupa & Co
15 Bankim Chatterjee Street, Calcutta 700 073
135 South Malaka, Allahabad 211 001
P. G. Solanki Path, Lamington Road, Bombay 400 007
7/16 Ansari Road, Daryaganj, New Delhi 110 002

Cover designed by S. Karmakar

Typeset in 9/10 Baskerville by
Megatechnics
19A Ansari Road
New Delhi 110 002

Printed in India by
Gopsons Papers Pvt Ltd
A-28, Sector IX
Noida 201 301

Rs 30

ISBN 81-7167-094-6

To

Dr. G.P. PHONDKE

who has inspired me through his writings

CONTENTS

Preface ix
Acknowledgements x
1. Sex and Sexuality through the Ages 11
2. Anatomy of Sex 16
3. Physiology of Sex 19
4. Sex Facts and Sex Myths 21
5. Famous Doctors of Sex 23
6. Sex Goddesses and Some Gods 25
7. Love Stories I 30
8. Love Stories II 32
9. Sex Disorders 36
10. Aphrodisiacs 38
11. Love Lives of Famous Men 42
12. Love Lives of Famous Women 46
13. Superlatives of Sex 47
14. Sexual Aberrations and Perversions 48
15. Famous Books and Magazines of Sex 57
16. Strange Customs 63
17. Sex Scandals 70
18. Sex Killings 73
19. Sexual Activities in Animals 75
20. Quotable Quotes 76
21. Sexually Transmitted Diseases 91
22. Hazy Areas 93
23. Slang and Euphemism 94
24. Movies 97
25. Legendary Creatures 99
26. The Laws 100
27. Great Sensualists 101
28. Arts and Entertainment 104

29. Easy Virtue 113
30. Potpourri 121
31. Picture Quiz 131
32. Bonus 133

ANSWERS 137

PREFACE

After the Green and the White Revolutions, India seems to be passing through a blue revolution now. Sex seems to be oozing out of everywhere — public hoardings, clubs, films, magazines, and even advertisements. However, many aspects of this interesting subject are largely unknown. This book is an attempt to present those little known, but highly interesting aspects of love and sex.

Perhaps for the first time, a book on love and sex has been written in a quiz format. It tests the awareness of the general reader on matters of love and sex. It can be used profitably by quiz masters who are looking for questions on love and sex to add spice to their quiz shows. Students of science can read the book to learn many interesting scientific facts on sex. An ordinary armchair reader would find interesting questions on virtually every aspect of sex, ranging from the history of sex and sexual customs to the interesting *bon mots* uttered by celebrities on sex.

As all quiz books are, this book is perhaps like a packet of popcorn which anybody can have in any dose at any time. If, besides amusing and entertaining the reader, this book is also able to create in them some awareness of matters of love and sex, its purpose will be served.

New Delhi

Anil Aggrawal

ACKNOWLEDGEMENTS

I wish to thank Ravindra Saxena of Butterworths who encouraged me to write this book. My elder brother, Pradeep, looked after all my personal affairs leaving me ample time to devote to this book. My younger brother, Sunil, encouraged me from across the country's frontiers. My special thanks are due to Mr. A. Habib Khan, Librarian, and Mr. S. U. Malik, Assistant Librarian, at the library of the Institute of History of Medicine at Hamdard Nagar. They let me pore over their vast collection of exotic books on sex, and sexual customs and such out-of-the-world books as *History of Prostitution.* Dr Prakash Kothari, Professor and Head of the Department of Sexual Medicine at G.S. Medical College K.E.M. Hospital, Bombay provided some interesting material — among them his highly readable book *Orgasm — New Dimensions.* Last but not the least I am thankful to my wife Aparna, who although I secretly suspect considered the subject somewhat smutty, yet not only let me go on with this book but provided some interesting information. Tarun as usual, suffered quietly and by now has learnt to say, 'Papa, I won't disturb you. I know you are writing yet another book.'

A.A.

1
SEX AND SEXUALITY THROUGH THE AGES

1. The most comprehensive laws governing sexual matters in ancient Greece were passed by

   (a) Alexander the Great (b) Philip of Macedon (c) Solon (d) Draco

2. Which famous man so successfully harried Margaret Sanger in her attempts to popularize birth control that she eventually fled to Europe, only returning after his death

   (a) President Eisenhower (b) Woodrow Wilson (c) John D. Rockefeller (d) Anthony Comstock

3. Which emperor issued an edict in 1495 declaring syphilis to be an affliction from God for the sins of men?

   (a) Emperor Maximilian (b) Ferdinand V (c) Henry VIII (d) Montezuma

4. Extracts of this plant were once used by society ladies to make themselves more attractive to men. They used the extract to make their eyes more lively. What is its name?

   (a) Rose (b) Touch-me-not (c) Deadly nightshade (d) Jasmine

5. Which famous physician said in A.D. 180, 'Watch carefully over this, young man; leave him alone neither day nor night; at least sleep in his chamber'?

   (a) Oribasius (b) Philumenos (c) Antyllus (d) Claudius Galen

6. The book *A Treatise on the Diseases Produced by Onanism,* was written by

   (a) the Swiss physician Simon Andre Tissot (b) the German-Canadian psychiatrist Karl Stern (c) the British physician Sir Richard Owen (d) the Anglo-Canadian physician Sir William Osler

7. From 1890 to 1925, there was a medical group in the United States which advocated and administered training in genital surgery for correction of the tendency to masturbate often. Name this group.

(a) The Anti-onanism society (b) Orificial Surgery Society (c) Society for the treatment of Masturbation (d) Gruppa onanismo curia

8. According to Assyrian laws, what was the punishment given to a man if he kissed the wife of another?

(a) Emasculation (b) Puncturing his eyes (c) Branding his cheeks with red hot iron (d) Cutting off the lower lip

9. According to Jewish law, how long after the birth of a daughter, could a woman engage again in sexual intercourse?

(a) 11 days (b) 33 days (c) 55 days (d) 101 days

10. According to Jewish law, if a husband died without heirs, his closest male relative was compelled to take the widow as a bride and provide her with children. What was this custom called?

(a) Levirate marriage (b) Widow marriage (c) Forced marriage (d) Sibling marriage

11. Which ancient lawmaker created state brothels called dicteria, which were run and taxed by the government?

(a) Alexander the Great (b) Caligula (c) Tiberius (d) Solon

12. In ancient Sparta, who encouraged pederasty as an important element in a boy's upbringing?

(a) Draco (b) Lycurgus (c) Philip of Macedonia (d) Theophrastus

13. Which English word came into being because of the strange practice of Roman prostitutes to solicit and entertain their customers waiting beneath arches?

(a) Fornicate (b) Cohabit (c) Copulate (d) Debauch

14. It is well known that the emperor Tiberius decorated his rooms with erotic frescoes. But there is one Roman poet also who is reputed to have done the same in his rooms. Who is he?

(a) Lucretius (b) Virgil (c) Horace (d) Catullus

15. Which Roman statesman was called by his contemporaries every woman's man and every man's woman?
(a) Julius Caesar (b) Augustus (c) Mark Antony (d) Nero

16. Which ancient physician reportedly used dummies in his lectures to apprentice physicians to demonstrate the roles of men and women in sexual activity?
(a) Galen (b) Avicenna (c) Charak (d) Hippocrates

17. What, in the nineteenth century, was referred to as the 'sport of venus'?
(a) Dancing naked with members of opposite sex (b) Bathing with a member of the opposite sex (c) Sexual intercourse (d) Lying naked in the sun

18. Which sexual position was advocated by the Christian missionaries to the natives of Polynesia?
(a) Man on top (b) Woman on top (c) Both lying side by side (d) Rear entry

19. Who founded the notorious Hellfire Club, with headquarters at Medmenham Abbey by the Thames, where members dressed as monks practised black magic and indulged in orgies with prostitutes dressed as nuns?
(a) Jan Cremer (b) Casanova (c) Felicien Rops (d) Sir Francis Dashwood

20. Which Christian apostle is widely held responsible for the Church's guilt-ridden and inhibited view of sex?
(a) St Bartholomew (b) St. Paul (c) St. Augustine (d) St. John Chrysostom

21. Which plant with a man-shaped root, and widely believed to have aphrodisiac powers, was also known as Satan's apple?
(a) Thinanthus (b) Tinospora (c) Fern (d) Mandrake

22. Which ancient Roman fertility festival was held annually on 23 February?
(a) Bacchanalia (b) Satyria (c) Lupercalia (d) Julia amora

23. In the late eighteenth and nineteenth centuries London ladies' directories were very popular. What were they?

(a) Printed lists of prostitutes (b) Price lists of diaphragms used for contraception (c) Directory of interesting sexual practices (d) Catalogues of beauty products

24. In seventeenth-century Spain and nineteenth-century China only a husband could ever see this part of female anatomy. Name it.

(a) Neck (b) Breasts (c) Pudenda (d) Feet

25. During whose reign in England, was it customary for young unmarried girls to expose their breasts up to the nipples as a sign of virginity?

(a) George III (b) James I (c) David II (d) William the Lion

26. Which club's proud mascot was a wig made from the pubic hair of king Charles II's mistresses?

(a) Mohawks (b) Wig Club (c) Dancing Club (d) The Gallants

27. Which Scottish club, founded in 1732, specialized in communal masturbation?

(a) The Honest Toilers (b) Dancing Club (c) Beggar's Benison (d) The Ticklers

28. Which ancient Roman erotic festival was held in mid-December?

(a) Agrionia (b) Floralia (c) Dionysia (d) Saturnalia

29. Who introduced permanent marriages in Greece?

(a) Cecrops (b) Xerxes II (c) Solon (d) Draco

30. Why did the ancient Romans deform the genitals of singers of both sexes?

(a) To propitiate Aphrodite (b) To propitiate Priapus (c) To ensure that their voices remained mellifluous (d) To punish them because singing in ancient Rome was considered profane

31. These ancient people carried carved phalli as good-luck amulets and placed them at crossroads and city gates and outside houses for protection. Who were these people?

(a) Greeks (b) Romans (c) Assyrians (d) Both Greeks and Romans

32. In ancient Rome, annual processions in honour of this god featured huge model penises carried by six men who themselves wore larger-than-life artificial dildos. Who was this god?

    (a) Hercules (b) Zeus (c) Pegasus (d) Liber

33. It was built on Seraglio Point, Constantinople, by Muhammad II in 1459-65, and was the model of all harems. What was it called?

    (a) Topkapi (b) El Kelmoune (c) El mokabeul (d) El tseguil

34. What were the white-slave brothels of America called, during eighteenth and nineteenth centuries?

    (a) Mares' Nests (b) Riding Schools (c) Kilambos (d) Harlots' Hostels

35. In ancient Greece what was the most significant gift which one lover could give to other?

    (a) A green twig (b) Apples (c) A gold chain (d) A flower vase

36. On which Greek island stood a temple of Apollo, from where a leap into the Ionian sea was supposed to confer immortality to lovers?

    (a) Delos (b) Milos (c) Mentos (d) Leucadia

37. In which country did the modern nudist movement start?

    (a) Germany (b) Czechoslovakia (c) U.S.A. (d) Sweden

38. Which among the following formed a nude bathing club on the shores of a reservoir near London in 1929?

    (a) Sun Ray Club (b) New Health Society (c) Birthday Suit Club (d) Freedom from Clothes Group

39. In ancient Babylon why was one of the temple prostitutes required to sleep each night in the top chamber of the Tower of Babel?

    (a) To guard it against thieves (b) To raise money by prostitution each night and offer it to the temple authorities the next day (c) To enable god Marduk to enjoy a woman in case he wanted to come in human shape (d) To give her some much-needed rest

40. In which ancient society could an elderly husband having a young wife, 'adopt' a younger man to father his children for him?

(a) Incas (b) Eskimos (c) Zulus (d) Spartans

2

ANATOMY OF SEX

Male

41. What is the length of each adult human testis?

(a) 1-2 cm (b) 2-$3\frac{1}{2}$ cm (c) $3\frac{1}{2}$-5 cm (d) 5-7 cm

42. During fetal development testes lie in the

(a) Chest (b) Abdomen (c) Penis (d) Scrotum

43. Just before birth testicles descend into the scrotum. Which testicle descends first?

(a) Left (b) Right (c) Both descend at the same time (d) In 50% people the left descends first and in the other 50% the right descends first

44. In what percentage of men do the testicles fail to descend completely, requiring surgical or hormonal treatment?

(a) 2% (b) 6% (c) 10% (d) 20%

45. In a rare condition, fluid collects around the testes, sometimes giving the appearance that there are three balls in the scrotum. What is this condition called?

(a) Hernia (b) Hydrocele (c) Orchitis (d) Cryptorchism

46. In men, the top of the pubic hair terminates in

(a) a straight line (b) an inverted-U (c) an inverted V (d) a curved line

47. What is the approximate length of a normal human penis when erect?

(a) 6 inches (b) 10 inches (c) 9 inches (d) 12 inches

48. In each human male, there are two pea-sized glands, lying near the root of the penis, which secrete a mucus-like material as part of the seminal fluid. What are these glands called?

(a) Cowper's glands (b) Bartholin's glands (c) Scarpa's glands (d) Vesalius' glands

49. What is the function of the Cremasteric muscle?

(a) Emission of semen (b) Erection of penis (c) Elevation of testes (d) They are vestigial muscles and thus have no function at all

50. Normally seminal fluid is stored in

(a) Testes (b) Prostate (c) Vas defrens (d) Seminal vesicles

51. The duct through which seminal fluid is propelled during the orgasm is known as

(a) Ureter (b) Urethra (c) Seminiferous tubules (d) Ductules

52. Which portion of male anatomy is colloquially known as 'the fireman's helmet'?

(a) The penis (b) The scrotum (c) The navel (d) The glans

53. How many sperms does an average man ejaculate in his lifetime?

(a) 2.5 billion (b) 100 billion (c) 1.5 trillion (d) 4.5 quadrillion

54. What is commonly referred to as Polymastia?

(a) A woman having more than two breasts (b) A woman having more than two nipples (c) A woman having a cluster of tiny nipples (d) A woman having many warts on her breasts

55. What is commonly referred to as Polythelia?

(a) Conical breasts (b) More than two nipples (c) Absence of sex organs in a woman (d) Presence of two uteri in a woman

56. What is the largest number of supernumerary nipples ever observed in one person?

(a) Five (b) Ten (c) Fifteen (d) Twenty

57. What percentage of human population is affected by polythelia or polymastia?

(a) .01% (b) 0.1% (c) 1% (d) 5%

58. An ill-defined area in female anatomy, comprising the whole of external genitalia is called

(a) Vagina (b) Hymen (c) Clitoris (d) Vulva

59. Thick folds of skin covering the vaginal opening are known as

(a) Labia majora (b) Fossa navicularis (c) Labia minora (d) Bartholin's folds

60. Two smaller folds of skin inside the Labia majora are called

(a) Labia submajora (b) Labia superminora (c) Labia minora (d) None of the above

61. Which structure of female anatomy is also known as nymphae?

(a) Labia majora (b) Labia minora (c) Hymen (d) Vagina

62. What is the name given to the pad of fatty tissue that surmounts a woman's pubic bone in front?

(a) Mons veneris (b) Hymen (c) Fourchette (d) Pelvic diaphragm

63. At what age do pubic hair start appearing in women?

(a) 5 years (b) 11 years (c) 17 years (d) 21 years

64. In women the top of the pubic hair terminates in a

(a) straight line (b) semicircle (c) inverted W (d) inverted U

65. What is the name given to an erectile organ of the female external genitalia that is the centre of sexual feeling and stimulation?

(a) Peniscule (b) Fourchette (c) Perineal body (d) Clitoris

66. What is the name of given to a membrane partially obstructing the vaginal opening in virgins?

(a) Fourchette (b) Perineum (c) Urethra (d) Hymen

67. The female nipple is sorrounded by a circular pigmented zone which is known as

(a) erotic area (b) areola (c) areata (d) Bartholin's gland

68. This pair of mucus-secreting glands have openings on either side of the lower part of the inner lips of the vagina. They are supposed to lubricate the vagina during sexual stimulation. What are these glands known as?

(a) Paraurethral glands (b) Tarsal glands (c) Bartholin's glands (d) Glands of Meibomeus

69. After menopause, the ovaries

(a) shrink (b) enlarge (c) remain unchanged in size (d) disappear altogether

70. The human ovum was first discovered by

(a) Sir Andrew Balfour (b) Robert Barany (c) Sir Frederick Grant Banting (d) Karl Ernst Ritter von Baer

71. To which part of the female anatomy did the victorians euphemistically refer to as 'Cupid's Arbour' or 'the Grove of Eglantine'?

(a) The cleft between breasts (b) Pubic hair (c) The cleft between the buttocks (d) The areola

3

PHYSIOLOGY OF SEX

72. How many spermatozoa are released in each human ejaculation?

(a) 1,000-5,000 (b) Ten thousand to one million (c) One million to a hundred million (d) 200 million to 400 million

73. Which hormone can restore virility to men who have lost their testicles?

(a) Testosterone (b) Progesterone (c) Lactate dehydrogenase (d) Corpus luteum

74. What is the state of penile erection or semi erection during sleep called?

(a) Venerism (b) Aphroditism (c) Erotic reverie (d) NPT

75. How much sleeping time does an average man spend in a state of penile erection?

(a) 5% (b) 25% (c) 50% (d) 75%

76. Testicles are kept at a temperature

(a) the same as that of body (b) 10°-15°F lower than that of the body (c) 10°-15°F higher than that of the body (d) varies according to sexual activity

77. The average blood loss during each menstrual period is

(a) 40 ml (b) 250 ml (c) 750 ml (d) more than 1 litre

78. How many menstrual periods does an average woman experience in her lifetime, if she remains childless?

(a) 101 (b) 301 (c) 440 (d) 950

79. When does ovulation normally occur in a woman?

(a) During menstrual bleeding (b) Just after menstrual bleeding (c) Just before menstrual bleeding (d) On the 14th day after the start of menstrual bleeding

80. During a woman's monthly cycle of ovulation, which is the least likely time for conception to occur?

(a) 14th day from the start of bleeding (b) the first 8 days and the last 8 days of the cycle (c) Only the first 8 days of the cycle (d) only the last 8 days of the cycle

81. What happens to the body temperature of a woman just at the time of ovulation?

(a) It reaches its lowest point (b) It rises sharply (c) It remains unchanged (d) It shows frequent changes

82. Which scientist first demonstrated that stimulation of the sacral nerves produced penile erection?

(a) Charles Scott Sherington (b) Wilhelm Wundt (c) Carl Eckhard (d) Claude Bernard

83. Women who have had one ovary surgically removed

(a) do not menstruate (b) do not conceive (c) suffer from scanty menstruation and conceive with extreme difficulty (d) remain normal as far as menstruation and power of conception are concerned

84. What percentage by weight of semen is water?

(a) 50% (b) 75% (c) 90% (d) 98%

85. Vasectomized men produce

(a) one-tenth of the normal amount of semen in each ejaculation (b) half the normal amount of semen (c) no semen at all (d) the normal amount of semen

86. During the beginning of life in a mother's womb all human embryos look female. During which week of life in mother's womb do the sex glands start differentiating into either ovaries or testes?

(a) 7th week (b) 15th week (c) 23rd week (d) 29th week

4
SEX FACTS AND SEX MYTHS

Some common beliefs about sex are given below. Tick (T) if they are true and (F) if they are false

87. Large labia minora in females is a sign of excessive masturbation. T/F
88. Sex during the middle of the menstrual cycle is more likely to produce babies. T/F
89. Excessive masturbation is a cause of stunted growth. T/F
90. Urinating in a bathroom, where a syphilitic patient has urinated before can cause syphilis. T/F
91. It is necessary to be able to give your wife an orgasm on the first night of sexual intercourse. T/F
92. Honey dissolved in milk arouses sexual desire; so it is desirable to drink this decoction before going to bed. T/F
93. Marriage among close relatives may result in deformed babies. T/F
94. Too much cigarette smoking may lead to impotence. T/F
95. Alcohol is an effective aphrodisiac. T/F
96. Cocaine will cure impotence in most cases. T/F
97. Most cases of impotence are psychological in origin and can be treated merely by reassurance. T/F
98. Too much sex may cause tuberculosis. T/F

99. If you find porn magazines in your teenage child's bed, it means they are in bad company. T/F

100. Taking contraceptive pills daily may cause cancer of the breast. T/F

101. You should not talk about sex to your child since he may then always think of sex. T/F

102. If a male marries an older female his sexual potency may be affected. T/F

103. Since I have had a vasectomy operation done, I can never have babies even if I want to. T/F

104. Since I get a desire to masturbate too often, I am abnormal and different from other boys. T/F

105. Semen is a storehouse of energy and so one should conserve it. T/F

106. Visiting prostitutes can give rise to sexually transmitted diseases such as syphilis and gonorrhoea. T/F

107. AIDS is an incurable disease. T/F

108. A ruptured hymen means that the wife is not a virgin. T/F

109. An old person above 60 years of age cannot produce a child. T/F

110. Since my penis is small, I shall be a poor sex partner. T/F

111. My wife is pregnant and the swelling on her abdomen is more on the right side, so it must be a boy. Had the swelling been on the left side, it would have been a girl. T/F

112. An X-chromosome-bearing gamete, on combining with another X-chromosome-bearing gamete will always produce a girl. T/F

113. If a condom is put on before visiting a prostitute, the chances of acquiring sexually transmitted diseases are much less. T/F

114. Trichomoniasis, an irritating vaginal infection, can be caught from a lavatory seat as well as from contaminated towels, flannels or clothing. T/F

115. Bleeding always occurs during a woman's first intercourse, so if on the wedding night, bleeding

doesn't occur, it means the bride has had sexual relations before. T/F

116. It is harmful to the man or the woman or both to have sexual intercourse during menstruation. T/F

117. The diaphragm by itself is *not* a satisfactory means of birth control. T/F

118. Powdered rhinoceros horn is the best aphrodisiac. T/F

119. It takes a woman 28 days to manufacture an ovum (an egg). T/F

120. Sexuality begins at puberty. T/F

121. Transvestites are homosexuals. T/F

122. You can have an ejaculation without an erection. T/F

123. There's no way a man can tell if a woman has had an orgasm or not. If she wants to fake it, she can always get away with it. T/F

5
FAMOUS DOCTORS OF SEX

124. At the age of two or three, this famous psychologist saw his mother in the nude, an event which aroused his young desires and played a leading role in the formation of his theories on sexuality. Who was this famous psychologist?

(a) Alfred Adler (b) Sigmund Freud (c) William James (d) Carl Gustav Jung

125. Which famous sexologist wrote the book *'Studies in the Psychology of Sex'*?

(a) Havelock Ellis (b) Sigmund Freud (c) Masters and Johnson (d) Alfred Charles Kinsey

126. He was a famous American biologist, sexologist and pioneer statistician of sexual behaviour, but he took a Ph.D. in entomology at Harvard. Who was he?

(a) Phyllis Kronhausen (b) Eberhard Kronhausen (c) Alfred Charles Kinsey (d) William H. Masters

127. Which Dutch gynaecologist was the author of the bestselling sex manual *Ideal Marriage* (1926)?

(a) Theodoor Hendrik Van de Velde (b) Tobias Michael Carel (c) Heike Kamerlingh-Onnes (d) Van der Waals

128. Which surgeon used to perform costly testicle transplants from apes to human males as a rejuvenation treatment?

(a) Ambrose Paré (b) Voronoff (c) Galen (d) Susruta

129. Who is reputed to be the first doctor to give frank and authoritative answers to sex problems in print?

(a) Dr Prakash Kothari (b) Dr Ambroise Paré (c) Dr Hip Pocrates (d) Dr Albert Schweitzer

130. When this famous French physiologist reached the age of seventytwo in 1889, he tried to rejuvenate himself by injecting mashed testicles of dogs and guinea pigs in a salt solution. Who was he?

(a) Henri Bergson (b) Leon Victor Auguste Bourgeois (c) Alexis Carrel (d) Charles Edouard Brown-Séquard

131. Who, in his excellent study *The Outer Fringe of Sex* points out that rubber fetishism is usually part of a syndrome that includes a liking for the feeling of protectedness and loss of identity that wearing rubber affords?

(a) Dr. Maurice North (b) Eric Berne (c) Sigmund Freud (d) Alfred Adler

132. Which famous Indian doctor was named 'Man of the year in the Field of Sexology' by the World Association for Sexology in December, 1989?

(a) Dr Padmavati (b) Dr A.S. Paintal (c) Dr. Prakash Kothari (d) Dr. Ramalingaswami

133. Which psychiatrist in his book *The Unconscious Significance of Hair* (1951) argues that untidy upstanding hair are socially unacceptable because they represent the erect penis?

(a) H.J. Eysenck (b) Eric Berne (c) Carl Rogers (d) Charles Berg

134. Which specialist in genitourinary disorders wrote a book on prostitution in 1857, which led to the Contagious Diseases Act, 1866 providing that prostitutes in garrison towns or naval depots should be subject to regular medical examination?

(a) Pedro Manuel de Almeida Lima (b) William Acton (c) Jules Bordet (d) Hermann Boerhaave

6

SEX GODDESSES AND SOME GODS

135. Who is the Greek goddess of love and beauty?
(a) Artemis (b) Ceres (c) Minerva (d) Aphrodite

136. Who is the Roman goddess of love and beauty?
(a) Proserpina (b) Venus (c) Anansi (d) None of the above

137. Who is the Indian goddess of love and beauty?
(a) Sri (b) Kali (c) Indrani (d) Parvati

138. Which Syrian god is represented by a conical black phallus?
(a) Ra (b) Baal (c) Chicomecoatl (d) Xiuhtectutli

139. Which Indian god is sometimes represented only by a black phallus?
(a) Vishnu (b) Brahma (c) Indra (d) Shiva

140. Who is the Indian god of love and desire?
(a) Indra (b) Kama (c) Brahma (d) Brihaspati

141. Who is the Indian goddess of passion?
(a) Rati (b) Usha (c) Parvati (d) Lakshmi

142. Which Egyptian god used to clutch his penis while taking an oath?
(a) Ares (b) Baal (c) Ra (d) Osiris

143. Who is the Mesopotamian goddess of fertility?
(a) Mithra (b) Ishtar (c) Khepri (d) Ra

144. Who is the Phoenician goddess of fertility?
(a) Astarte (b) Athena (c) Tiamat (d) Tvashtri

145. Who is the Canaanite goddess of fertility?
(a) Tantalus (b) Sphinx (c) Anat (d) Geb

146. Who is the Greek god of marriage, who is usually represented as the tutelary god wearing a wreath or as a boy carrying a torch?
(a) Io (b) Hymen (c) Icarus (d) Daedalus

147. Who was the fertility god of the Hellespont region, whose cult spread to Greece and Alexandria in the third century B.C.?

(a) Priapus (b) Procrustes (c) Semele (d) Zephyrus

148. Which was the sacrificial animal of Priapus?

(a) Dog (b) Goat (c) Elephant (d) Donkey

149. Which fertility goddess made love to her husband so violently that it killed him?

(a) Rhea (b) Ishtar (c) Athena (d) Hera

150. Who in Greek legend fell in love with his own reflection in a pool?

(a) Nemesis (b) Muses (c) Narcissus (d) Dionysus

151. Which beautiful girl fell in love with Narcissus, but pined away when he was not interested, and only her voice was left?

(a) Echo (b) Rhea (c) Psyche (d) Persephone

152. Which of the following goddesses presides over childbirth?

(a) Eileithyia (b) Hera (c) Vesta (d) Zeuxis

153. Which English month has been named after the Greek goddess of love and beauty

(a) June (b) April (c) May (d) July

154. At the Rijks Museum in Amsterdam, Holland, there is an Egyptian coffin painting showing the goddess of the sky, Nut. Her mouth is described as the western horizon. Which part of her body is described as the eastern horizon?

(a) Anus (b) Feet (c) Perineum (d) Vulva

155. Which of the nine Greek muses is generally represented nude?

(a) Melpomene (b) Clio (c) Terpsichore (d) Thalia

156. What was the sacred symbol of Ishtar?

(a) Hand holding a lotus (b) Vulva (c) Swan (d) Two pigeons in an act of billing

157. She was a concubine of Achilles, later forcibly taken away by Agamemnon. One of the platenoids is named after her. Who is she?

(a) Briseïs (b) Gunlöd (c) Zelinda (d) Melitta

158. Who is the Greek god of love?

(a) Cupid (b) Eros (c) Eteocles (d) Dionysus

159. Who is the Roman god of love?

(a) Nessus (b) Psyche (c) Pygmalion (d) Cupid

160. Which god of love, carrying a bow and an arrow, can be seen at the centre of the fountain in Piccadilly Circus in London?

(a) Kama (b) Eros (c) Cupid (d) Baal

161. Why is Cupid often depicted blindfolded?

(a) His lover Venus had blinded him in a fit of anger (b) He was born blind (c) It shows his victims are chosen at random (d) So that by his look he cannot corrupt too many maidens

162. Which famous sensuous woman was also known as the 'Swedish Sphinx'?

(a) Greta Garbo (b) Margaret of Sweden (c) Ingrid Bergman (d) Bibi Andersson

163. She was the star of silent pictures; personified It or sex appeal and thus came to be widely called the It Girl. Who was she?

(a) Marilyn Monroe (b) Racquel Welsh (c) Brigitte Bardot (d) Clara Bow

164. Which beautiful tennis player was offered $ 270,000 to pose in the nude for *Penthouse* magazine?

(a) Gabriela Sabatini (b) Steffi Graf (c) Monica Seles (d) Arantxa Sanchez

165. Which Chinese princess of the Sung Dynasty had a special bed made to her personal design so that 30 men could lie on it while she enjoyed them all?

(a) Li-chin (b) Fa-gin (c) Shan-yin (d) Yin-Yng

166. Which wife of Henry VIII had three breasts?

(a) Catherine Parr (b) Anne Boleyn (c) Catherine Howard (d) Anne of Cleves

167. Which of the following glamorous women bathed in asses's milk?

(a) Calpurnia (b) Livia (c) Agrippina II (d) Poppaea

168. Which of the following film actresses committed suicide?

(a) Rita Hayworth (b) Jane Fonda (c) Marilyn Monroe (d) Mae West

169. This sex symbol and actress was groomed by Carlo Ponti, who she later married. Who was she?

(a) Elizabeth Taylor (b) Sophia Loren (c) Liza Minelli (d) Bo Derek

170. She starred in Broadway until the police closed two of her plays *Sex* and *Pleasure Man* in 1928. Who was she?

(a) Mae West (b) Anne Sheridan (c) Clara Bow (d) Marilyn Monroe

171. An asteroid has been named after this Greek beauty, who was a concubine of Heracles. Who was she?

(a) Thia (b) Jole (c) Arachne (d) Ottilia

172. This celebrated actress and sex symbol has been married as many as eight times. Who is she?

(a) Mary Todd Lincoln (b) Sophia Loren (c) Mae West (d) Elizabeth Taylor

173. The above actress has been married to a total of seven men. Whom did she marry twice?

(a) Nicky Hilton (b) Michael Wilding (c) Richard Burton (d) John Warner

174. Elizabeth Taylor divorced all her husbands except one who actually died in an air crash. Who was he?

(a) Mike Todd (b) Eddie Fischer (c) John Warner (d) Nicky Hilton

175. Which of Taylor's husbands was heir to a multi-million-dollar hotel chain?

(a) Eddie Fischer (b) Nicky Hilton (c) John Warner (d) Richard Burton

176. Her friend, French writer Colette, said that her breasts 'were of curious shape, reminding one of elongated lemons, firm and upturned at the tips'. An anonymous source added that her breasts 'preceded her by a quarter of an hour'. Who was this buxon courtesan?

(a) Kitty Fisher (b) Billie Holliday (c) Harriette Wilson (d) La Belle Otero

177. She was the first actress in Hollywood to appear regularly in films without a bra. In fact she never liked wearing bras and when a high school teacher reprimanded her for this, she replied, 'I can't breathe when I'm wearing a brassière.' Who was this famous actress?

(a) Sophia Loren (b) Mae West (c) Jean Harlow (d) Anne Sheridan

178. Which US actress, largely because of her splendid legs, was known as the 'pin-up Girl'?

(a) Betty Grable (b) Mae West (c) Tallulah Bankhead (d) Clara Bow

179. Which famous lady, renowned for her flamboyant style, once celebrated the birthday of her husband, the English Prime Minister Lord Melbourne, by having herself served naked to him as a birthday banquet dish?

(a) Josephine Baker (b) Billie Holliday (c) Natalie Barney (d) Caroline Lamb

180. She was the heroine of the X-rated movie *Captain Lust*. When she experienced difficulty getting a cheque cashed, because of lack of proof of identity, she handed the teller a magazine containing a nude picture of herself. Who was this girl?

(a) Sharon Mitchell (b) Billie Holliday (c) Rita Hayworth (d) Mae West

181. Which famous striptease performer believed that "flesh bores men"?

(a) Gypsy Rose Lee (b) Madame de Pompadour (c) Miss Geri Miller (d) Stasia Napierkowska

182. Which famous woman, symbolizing sex, said, "I want the world to see my body"?

(a) Mae West (b) Sophia Loren (c) Marilyn Monroe (d) Rita Hayworth

183. She is an Australian-born academic and protagonist of women's liberation and the author of a best-selling book. She has been photographed in the nude for *Screw* magazine. Who is she?

(a) Kate Millet (b) Germaine Greer (c) Ninon de Lenclos (d) Katherine Mansfield

7

LOVE STORIES I

184. Every evening he swam across the strait to meet her, guided by a lamp which his lover lit on the top of a tower of the house in which she lived. One stormy night the lamp went out and his corpse was washed ashore the next day. Who was the unfortunate lover?

    (a) Leander (b) Hesiod (c) Pegasus (d) Nestor

185. Who was the lover of Eros?

    (a) Athena (b) Aphrodite (c) Psyche (d) Diana

186. Eros used to meet his lover only in darkness and even made her pregnant without her having seen him. Ultimately however she did light a lamp to see him. Why did she do it?

    (a) Zeus ordered her to do so (b) Her two sisters had convinced her that her lover was a monster and she wanted to make sure (c) She felt ashamed of having been impregnated by an unknown lover (d) Under a curse from Artemis, she would abort if she didn't see her lover

187. What happened to Eros, after he was thus seen by her lover?

    (a) He died (b) He became blind (c) He developed an abhorrence for his lover (d) He was scalded by a drop of hot oil falling on his shoulder and immediately flew away

188. Acontius had sworn by Artemis to marry her only. So whenever her father tried to marry her off somewhere else, she fell violently sick. Who was she?

    (a) Cydippe (b) Dido (c) Dictys (d) Cybele

189. Which Theban princess was loved by Zeus in the form of a satyr?

    (a) Andromache (b) Antigone (c) Antiope (d) Hera

190. She was an Arcadian goddess, and was one of the loves of Zeus. Artemis turned her into a bear as a punishment for not remaining a virgin, but Zeus immortalized her by placing her among the stars as the constellation of the Great Bear. Who was she?

    (a) Calypso (b) Callisto (c) Penelope (d) Sibylla

191. This Greek mountain nymph was the daughter of the river Peneius. Apollo took a fancy of her and chased her. Not wishing to give herself to him, she fled to the mountains and eventually asked mother Earth to change her into a laurel tree. Who was she?

(a) Daphne (b) Io (c) Europa (d) Ganymede

192. Cybele was the great mother-goddess of Phrygia. Who was her youthful lover?

(a) Zeus (b) Cronos (c) Apollo (d) Attis

193. Her father imprisoned her, in a bronze tower so that her lover Zeus couldn't meet her. Zeus got round the problem by visiting her in the form of a shower of gold. Who was she?

(a) Leda (b) Io (c) Danaë (d) Persephone

194. Which of his lovers was visited by Zeus in the form of a Swan?

(a) Leda (b) Ganymede (c) Europa (d) Io

195. Who was Zeus's wife, violently jealous of his many love-affairs?

(a) Clymnestera (b) Hera (c) Europa (d) Ganymede

196. Zeus loved this young girl from Argos very much, but to save her from the wrath of his wife, he turned her into a superb white heifer. Who was she?

(a) Metis (b) Adrastea (c) Ananke (d) Io

197. She was Zeus's grand-daughter's grand-daughter, yet Zeus took a fancy of her and visited her disguised in the form of a snowwhite bull. Who is she?

(a) Sinope (b) Pasiphaë (c) Europa (d) Himalia

198. Zeus was so over-sexed that he even had intercourse with his sisters. Which of his sisters gave birth to Persephone after union with him?

(a) Demeter (b) Mnemosyne (c) Athena (d) Themis

8
LOVE STORIES II

199. Who wrote the best-selling novel *Love Story* in 1970?
(a) Jacqueline Susan (b) Erich Segal (c) A.B. Yehoshva (d) Eudora Welty

200. What was the sequel of *Love Story* called?
(a) *Oliver's Story* (b) *Love Poems* (c) *Love Story II* (d) There was no sequel

201. Which popular historical romance was the 1937 Pulitzer Prize winner?
(a) *Lolita* (b) *Sons and Lovers* (c) *Lady Chatterley's Lover* (d) *Gone with the Wind*

202. In which famous love story does the heroine marry Angel Clare after she had been raped by an unscrupulous person?
(a) *The Seagull* (b) *Rebecca* (c) *Tess of the D'Urbervilles* (d) *A Good Woman*

203. This epistolary novelette by Goethe, about a sentimental love-affair, plunged all Europe into tears, and made suicide for love fashionable among the young. Name the novel.
(a) *The Sorrows of Young Werther* (b) *Faust* (c) *Egmont* (d) *Torquato Tasso*

204. Which poem by Lord Byron extolled incestuous love between the beautiful Zuleika and her brother Selim?
(a) *The Corsair* (b) *Lara* (c) *Don Juan* (d) *The Bride of Abydos*

205. In which Shakespearean play do we find the beautiful Desdemona?
(a) *King Lear* (b) *Macbeth* (c) *Hamlet* (d) *Othello*

206. Who is Miranda's lover in *The Tempest*?
(a) *Prospero* (b) *Ferdinand* (c) *Ariel* (d) *Antonio*

207. Psychiatrists sometimes speak of the Othello syndrome. What does this mean?
(a) Delusions of infidelity (b) Delusions of grandeur (c) Delusions of reference (d) Colour-inferiority complex

208. In *Measure for Measure*, who is Claudio's beloved?

(a) *Isabella* (b) *Juliet* (c) *Marina* (d) *Francisca*

209. In *A Midsummer Night's Dream* who is in love with Lysander?

(a) Hippolyta (b) Helena (c) Hermia (d) Titania

210. In which city does the action of *The Taming of the Shrew* take place?

(a) Florence (b) Pisa (c) Rome (d) Padua

211. In *Twelfth Night* who does Sir Toby Belch marry?

(a) Maria (b) Viola (c) Olivia (d) One who belches doesn't get married

212. In *The Merchant of Venice* who does Shylock's daughter run away with?

(a) Solanio (b) Salerio (c) Launcelet (d) Lorenzo

213. In *Much Ado About Nothing* who tries to cross the proposed marriage of Claudio with Hero?

(a) Borachio (b) Antonio (c) Dogberry (d) Benedick

214. Who is the Shrew in Shakespeare's play who has to be tamed?

(a) Bianca (b) Katherina (c) Jaquenetta (d) Adriana

215. 'Go ask his name — If he be married,
My grave is like to be my wedding bed.'
Who says this of whom in Shakespeare?

(a) Sylvania, of Valentine (b) Miranda, of Ferdinand (c) Juliet, of Romeo (d) Rosalind, of Orlando

216. Identify the mismatched pair.

(a) Rosalind and Orlando (b) Florizel and Perdita (c) Imogen and Posthumus (d) Orsino and Olivia

217. On which time-tested principle is the shrew tamed in *The Taming of a Shrew*?

(a) Enlist the mother-in-law's goodwill (b) Kill the cat on the first night of wedding (c) Pretend to be afraid of your wife (d) Do not open your mouth at all

218. In which Shakespearean play do we meet the twin brother and sister Sebastian and Viola?

(a) *The Tempest* (b) *Measure for Measure* (c) *Twelfth Night* (d) *Romeo and Juliet*

219. With whom does Viola fall in love?

(a) Duke Orsino (b) Pericles (c) Sebastian (d) Sir Toby Belch

220. Whom does Duke Orsino love?

(a) Viola (b) Olivia (c) Maria (d) None of the above

221. Who ultimately marries Olivia?

(a) Duke Orsino (b) Sebastian (c) Toby Belch (d) Sir Andrew Aguecheek

222. Which female wears male attire in *Twelfth Night* and creates a lot of confusion?

(a) Maria (b) Nadia (c) Viola (d) Olivia

223. In which Shakespearean play do we meet the characters Valentine and Proteus?

(a) *The Two Gentlemen of Verona* (b) *Cymbeline* (c) *As You Like It* (d) *Measure for Measure*

224. Who does Valentine love?

(a) Julia (b) Nadia (c) Belia (d) Silvia

225. Who does Proteus love initially?

(a) Julia (b) Nadia (c) Belia (d) Silvia

226. Silvia's father, the Duke of Milan, wants that Silvia should marry

(a) Valentine (b) Proteus (c) Thurio (d) None of the above

227. Who does Silvia finally marry?

(a) Valentine (b) Proteus (c) Thurio (d) She remains unmarried

228. In which Shakespearean play do we meet the beautiful Imogen?

(a) *Much Ado About Nothing* (b) *The Comedy of Errors* (c) *The Taming of the Shrew* (d) *Cymbeline*

229. At 37, this theologian, poet, and teacher became involved in a passionate love affair with Héloise, a beautiful and brilliant girl of 17 whom he was tutoring. Who was he?

(a) Alcaeus (b) Nicander of Xenophon (c) Peter Abélard (d) Sir Francis Dashwood

230. When his mistress, Marguerite de Bonnemain died of tuberculosis in 1891, he had her tombstone

inscribed with this simple message, 'Marguerite. See you soon.' Who was this ardent lover?

(a) Georges Ernest Boulanger (b) Dominique Bouhours (c) Borso d' Este (d) Phil Esposito

231. William Earl Pearson, a Texas doctor, performed an emergency appendectomy on her during the filming of *Dangerous Curves.* Their love grew so much that they wanted to marry but the good doctor's wife filed a suit against her. Who was this famous actress?

(a) Gina Lollobrigida (b) Zsa Zsa Gabor (c) Lucille Ball (d) Clara Bow

232. In the famous love story of Sassi-Punnu, who was Punnu?

(a) A beggar (b) The Prince of Kutch (c) A washerman (d) A carpenter

233. Just as Taj Mahal was built by Shahjehan for his queen Mumtaz Mahal, the hanging gardens of Babylon were built by King Nebuchadnezzar for his beloved queen. Who was she?

(a) Queen Alexandra (b) Queen Memphis (c) Queen Amytis (d) Queen Hatshepsut

234. Which Byzantine king married a prostitute in defiance of a law prohibiting aristocrats to marry prostitutes?

(a) Justinian I (b) Heraclius I (c) Constans II (d) Philippicus

235. His earliest love was Florrie Balcombe whom he met when he was 21, but she preferred to marry Bram Stoker, the author of *Dracula,* leaving him heartbroken. Who was he?

(a) T.E. Lawrence (b) Oscar Wilde (c) William Gladstone (d) Dwight David Eisenhower

9

SEX DISORDERS

236. Pruritis vulvae is a disorder in which there is

(a) reddening of the genitals (b) itching in female genitals (c) itching in male genitals (d) foul smelling discharge from the male genitals

237. Which vaginal infection causes profuse yellowish green irritating discharge and also itching and swelling of the vulva?

(a) Trichomoniasis (b) Moniliasis (c) AIDS (d) Any of the above

238. Trichomoniasis is caused by a

(a) bacteria (b) virus (c) protozoon (d) insect

239. The term dyspareunia means

(a) extremely pleasurable intercourse (b) intercourse followed by vomiting (c) intercourse followed by severe itching in the genital organs (d) extremely painful intercourse

240. Persistent inability to obtain or maintain a penile erection suitable for sexual intercourse is known as

(a) sterility (b) infertility (c) impotence (d) spermatorrhoea

241. The best definition of sterility is

(a) inability to procreate or conceive children (b) inability to maintain an erection (c) inability to perform sexual intercourse (d) inability to achieve an orgasm

242. Which of the following sex disorders in a spouse gives a just cause for nullity of marriage to the other spouse?

(a) Impotence (b) Sterility (c) Enuresis (d) Priapism

243. Sometimes a man is persistently unable to perform sexual intercourse with just one woman — usually his wife, although he is quite capable of performing sexual intercourse with other women. What would this type of impotence be called?

(a) Psychogenic impotence (b) Functional impotence (c) Secondary impotence (d) Relative impotence

244. Which disease was once so common during honeymoon that it acquired the name of 'honeymoon disease'?

(a) Inflammation of breasts (b) Inflammation of labia minora (c) Inflammation of urinary bladder (d) Contusion of clitoris

245. There is a rare condition in which the hymen completely occludes the opening to the vagina, leaving no room for even menstrual blood to come out. What is this condition called?

(a) Septate hymen (b) Imperforate hymen (c) Annular hymen (d) Fimbriate hymen

246. Collection of menstrual blood within the vagina is called

(a) haemotocele (b) hydrocele (c) haematocolpos (d) haemorrhoids

247. Balanitis is the name given to the inflammation of

(a) breast (b) penis (c) clitoris (d) either penis or clitoris

248. Lack of sexual desire in males is called

(a) Alarsenia (b) Vernalagnia (c) Apistia (d) Emeronaria

249. Gynecomastia is a disorder in which

(a) a female developes three breasts (b) a female develops multiple breasts (c) breasts develop at a very early age (d) males develop breasts

250. An anomaly of the penis where the orifice of the foreskin is too small for it to be retracted is known as

(a) paraphimosis (b) phimosis (c) Peyronie's disease (d) Valsalva's disease

251. Which king of France suffered from the above disorder?

(a) Henri I (b) Philip II (c) Louis XVI (d) John I

252. Which disease results in a badly bent penis, because of which its popular name is 'the bent-nail syndrome'?

(a) Peyronie's disease (b) Syphilis (c) Lymphogranuloma venerum (d) Leprosy

253. Some men are able to score only with their wives. What are they called?

(a) Narcissists (b) Uxoravalent (c) Sanctimonists (d) Uxorovalent

10
APHRODISIACS

254. The word aphrodisiac comes from

(a) a Chinese word meaning love (b) the name of a Greek goddess of love and beauty (c) a Balinese word meaning 'sex-food' (d) a potent plant called aphrodita.

255. Australian aborigines drink a beverage made up of corkwood, which is supposed to give them strong erotic sensations. What is the active consistuent of corkwood?

(a) Hyoscine (b) Duboisine (c) Hyoscyamine (d) Brucine

256. This plant is supposed to be an aphrodisiac. The Chinese call it the "elixir of life". Which is this plant?

(a) Ginseng (b) Cocaine (c) Avena sativa (d) Cannabis

257. What are the active principles of Ginseng?

(a) Brucine (b) Strychnine (c) Saponin glycosides (d) Panaxosides

258. This metallic green-coloured insect is perhaps the most celebrated aphrodisiac. Name it.

(a) Stick insect (b) Green locust (c) Spanish fly (d) Silkworm cocoon

259. What was recommended by Hippocrates, the father of medicine, as an aphrodisiac?

(a) Amyl nitrate (b) Cakes made from asses' milk and honey (c) Grass mixed with opium (d) A decoction of honey and minced rose rubbed on genital organs

260. On April 26, 1954, 44 year old Arthur Kendrick Ford gave this aphrodisiac to two young girls, thinking they would come flying into his arms. They died instead and Ford got five years. Which was this aphrodisiac?

(a) Ginseng (b) Cocaine (c) Royal jelly (d) Spanish Fly

261. This viscous substance secreted from the pharyngeal glands of worker honey bees is meant to be used locally for its aphrodisiac action. Name it.

(a) Bee glue (b) Royal Jelly (c) Worker bee putty (d) Mucilage

262. Which vitamin is supposed to act as a sex tonic?

(a) Vitamin A (b) Vitamin K (c) Vitamin D (d) Vitamin E

263. Galen, Ovid and Sheikh Nefzawi believed that this substance has outstanding aphrodisiac powers. What is it?

(a) Pearls (b) Ashes of gold (c) Honey (d) Lobster

264. This substance has been praised as an aphrodisiac by such notable personalities as Rabelais, Casanova, George Sand, Sade, Napoleon and Mme Pompadour. Name this substance.

(a) Truffles (b) Peaches (c) Garlic (d) Eel

265. This has been described as an aphrodisiac by Henry Fielding in his book *Tom Jones.* Name it.

(a) Ginseng (b) Lobster (c) Eel meat (d) Oysters

266. Casanova called them "a spur to the spirit and to love". They are one of the most renowned aphrodisiac foods. Name them.

(a) Oysters (b) Chimpanzee's breasts (c) Cola nuts (d) Basil leaves

267. Herbalist Nicholas Culpeper (1616-54) wrote, 'this fruit provokes lust.' The Chinese considered the fruit's sweet juices symbolic of the effluvia of the vagina. Which fruit are we talking about?

(a) Oranges (b) Mango (c) Grapes (d) Peaches

268. This vegetable which is widely considered to be aphrodisiac contains rich quantities of potassium, phosphorus and calcium — all necessary for maintenance of a high energy level. It also contains an amino acid aspartic acid. Name this vegetable.

(a) Cabbage (b) Cucumber (c) Asparagus (d) Radish

269. This drug, usually prescribed for heart pain, is used by some individuals as an aphrodisiac, who inhale it just before orgasm. Which is it?

(a) Digitalis (b) Amyl nitrite (c) Pilocarpine (d) Pethidine

270. This greyish substance, now chiefly used in perfumery, was once widely used as an aphrodisiac, especially in Arabian, Indian and Chinese medicines. Name this substance.

(a) Amaranthus (b) Asparagus (c) Ambergris (d) Sweet Flag

271. This greenish liquor contains the oil of wormwood. Its occasional use can be extremely stimulating and desirable, but a prolonged use can even damage sexual powers. Name this substance.

(a) Absinthe (b) Toad venom (c) Juice of *dhatura* (d) Juice of opium

272. This brown or black foamy substance, which sometimes appears upon the forehead of a newborn foal was once used by the ancient Romans as an aphrodisiac. Name it.

(a) Heirba del Chive (b) Hibiscus (c) Hippomanes (d) Supplejack

273. According to the Bible, Rachel, the younger of the two wives of Jacob, wanted to have this plant because it would make her more fertile and because it was reputed to be sexually stimulating. Which is this plant?

(a) Mandrake (b) Malay Pea (c) Polypodium (d) Poqe

274. It was one of the gifts of the Magi to newborn Jesus. Ancient Hebrews considered it a great aphrodisiac. Its botanical name is *Commiphora molmol.* How is it more commonly known?

(a) Frankincense (b) Myrrh (c) Mistletoe (d) Wormwood

275. This plant of the Mallow family, native to the East Indies and other parts of Asia, was supposed to be useful in restoring the penile powers of a man who was in his eightieth year. Its botanical name is *Hibiscus moschatus*. Name this plant.

(a) Nandina (b) Holy Thistle (c) Sumbul (d) Musk

276. This nonprescription drug, chemically related to amyl nitrite, and equally dangerous, is supposed to be an aphrodisiac and sold in the United States as 'liquid incense'. Name this drug.

(a) Propyl nitrite (b) Butaraldehyde (c) Isobutyl nitrite (d) Alkyl nitrite

277. The botanical name of this plant is *Glycyrrhiza echinata*. It contains the female sex hormone estrogen and according to ancient belief, a woman who chews it will become passionate. Name the plant.

(a) Licorice (b) Cuscuta (c) Tinospora (d) Native Sarsaparilla

278. Normally this drug is prescribed for Parkinson's disease, but it has been known to augment the sexual drive in many people. Name this drug.

(a) Benzedrine (b) L-DOPA (c) Nitrofurantoin (d) Nalidixic acid

279. This very dangerous aphrodisiac is made from the testes of the poisonous puffer fish. In Japan, between 250 and 300 individuals die each year after taking it. Name it.

(a) Gilo (b) Liquid amber (c) Fugu (d) Nandina

280. Many people consider it an aphrodisiac, but instead it may be called a long-term aid to general well-being. Russian astronauts took this drug to strengthen them in their hazardous ventures. Name this drug.

(a) Harmal (b) Siberian Ginseng (c) Kiev Nutmeg (d) Siberian Musk

281. Henry Kissinger called it the ultimate aphrodisiac. What is it?

(a) Spanish Fly (b) Love (c) Ginger beer (d) None of the above

282. Which popular aphrodisiac is made from the powdered inner bark of the African yohimbé tree?

(a) Yohimbodicene (b) Yohimbine (c) Yawine (d) African honey

283. Leaves of this Mexican shrub have been used as a mild sexual stimulant and also as a hallucinogenic medication. Name the shrub.

(a) Zacatechichi (b) Rubus (c) Purple sage (d) Rhododendron

11

LOVE LIVES OF FAMOUS MEN

284. Whenever he kissed his wife's or mistress's neck, he would whisper, 'Off comes this head whenever I give the word'. Who was he?

(a) Pope Alexander VI (b) Caligula (c) King Henry VIII (d) Ivan, the terrible

285. Which prominent Frenchman died while engaged in the sex act?

(a) Felix Faure (b) Charles de Gaulle (c) Marshal Pétain (d) Louis XIV

286. Which famous American poet, a homosexual, lived with a young Irish-American horse-bus conductor named Peter Doyle, addressing him in letters as 'my darling'?

(a) Nathaniel Hawthorne (b) William Faulkner (c) Ezra Pound (d) Walt Whitman

287. Which famous Nobel Peace Prize winner was a lover of the famous courtesan La Belle Otero? About him Otero recalled, 'once he made love to me eight times before morning. And he was 50 years old at the time.' Who is this Nobel Laureate?

(a) Aristide Briand (b) Sir Joseph Austen Chamberlain (c) Fridtjof Nansen (d) Leon Victor Auguste Bourgeois

288. Lady Caroline Lamb, the 27-year-old wife of William Lamb, who later became Lord Melbourne, Prime Minister of England, sent her lover a thatch of her pubic hair and a long note. Among other things it said, 'I cut the hair too close, and it bled. Do you not the same.' Who was this amorous lover?

(a) Percy Bysshe Shelley (b) John Keats (c) Lord Byron (d) Franz Joseph Haydn

289. About which great man did Kay Summersby Morgan, an aristocratic young Irish woman said, 'His kisses absolutely unravelled me. They are hungry, strong and demanding'?

(a) Adolf Hitler (b) Dwight David Eisenhower (c) Albert Einstein (d) Père Alexandre Dumas

290. This man of music used to write erotic letters to his pupil Countess Delfina Potocka. Once he wrote, 'I would like again to plop something down your little hole in D flat major.' Who was he?

(a) Frédéric François Chopin (b) Beethoven (c) Peter Tchaikovsky (d) Antonin Dvorak

291. His first love at 15 was Nelly Kirkpatrick, his partner in the traditional harvest festivities. She was the subject of the first poem he ever wrote, *Handsome Nell*. Who is this man?

(a) Ezra Pound (b) T.S. Eliot (c) W.B. Yeats (d) Robert Burns

292. Which famous tennis player once publicly claimed that he had made love to his girl friend in the men's locker room only minutes before a game at the Australian Open?

(a) Bjorn Borg (b) Jimmy Connors (c) Yannick Noah (d) Manuelo Santana

293. In 1953, while filming in Rome, he contracted hepatitis from a dirty needle. In hospital he kept his pecker up with the aid of twice-daily visits from a couple of streetwalkers who administred oral sex. Who was he?

(a) John Barrymore (b) Errol Flynn (c) Omar Sharief (d) Frank Sinatra

294. This famous king of Great Britain was known for the retinue of mistresses he kept. When his dying queen begged him to marry again he said, 'No, I shall have mistresses'. Who was he?

(a) James I (b) Henry VIII (c) William IV (d) George II

295. He was a lifelong connoisseur of bottoms and once fondly described his wife's rump as 'the prettiest little backside imaginable'. Who was he?

(a) Karl Marx (b) Charles Dickens (c) Johny Walker (d) Napoleon Bonaparte

296. Which famous king died on his wedding night?

(a) Attila, the Hun (b) John I of France (c) Charlemagne (d) Justinian II

297. Which Pope of the Roman Church died of a stroke while committing adultery?

(a) John XIV (b) Boniface VII (c) Innocent VI (d) Leo VIII

298. Which Roman head of state is reported to have dressed as a woman, to have depilated his body and facial hair and to have bathed with the women in the baths?

(a) Elagabalus (b) Nero (c) Hadrian (d) Domitian

299. During a visit to a government farm, this famous First Lady paused at a chicken pen to inquire of the overseer whether the rooster copulated more than once a day. When he answered, 'Dozens of times,' she said at once, 'Tell that to the President.' Who was this Lady?

(a) Mrs. Jimmy Carter (b) Mrs. Truman (c) Mrs. Reagan (d) Mrs. Coolidge

300. Which famous psychologist on a visit to the United States, admitted to his friend that he found American women disturbing and that they gave him erotic dreams?

(a) Alfred Adler (b) Carl Gustav Jung (c) Sigmund Freud (d) Eric Berne

301. On his proselytizing journeys, the Bible describes him as travelling with "a wife who was a sister to him." Who was this saintly man?

(a) Saint John (b) Pope Paul II (c) Saint Thomas Aquinas (d) Saint Paul

302. Which of the following authors suffered from syphilis?

(a) Guy de Maupassant (b) Socrates (c) Isaac Asimov (d) Henry Fielding

303. Caligula, the tyrant of Rome, was such a debauch that he had sexual congress even with all his sisters. He made one his official wife. Who was she?

(a) Caligenna (b) Drusilla (c) Pyxalites (d) Agrippa

304. About whom did Goethe write to a friend, 'But I love her. I believe I would take poison from her hand'?

(a) Virginia Woolf (b) Catherine the Great (c) Käthchen Schönkopf (d) Chopin's wife

305. This Romanian King was married to Princess Helen of Greece, but actually loved Magda Lupescu, the divorced daughter of a Jewish pharmacist. For her he even renounced the throne of Romania. Who was he?

(a) Ferdinand I (b) Alexander IV (c) Carol II (d) Philip III

306. At the age of fourteen, this French painter of Parisian night life broke both his legs and from then on ceased to grow. But he suffered from excessive development of the genitals which won him the nickname 'teapot'. Identify him.

(a) Henri de Toulouse-Lautrec (b) Jean Francois Millet (c) Gustave Courbet (d) Eugéne Delacroix

307. Which French writer could reportedly achieve an erection at will and to prove his virility, once took a witness to a brothel and had six girls in an hour?

(a) Honoré de Balzac (b) Voltaire (c) Denis Diderot (d) Guy de Maupassant

308. He was the first male pin-up featured in the English edition of *Cosmopolitan* magazine. For a brief period he was also the husband of the best-selling author Germaine Greer. Who is he?

(a) Georges Joseph Grassal (b) Paul de Feu (c) Hans Appel (d) Manfred Truber

309. Which famous king owned a wig of his mistresses' pubic hair as a sexual fetish?

(a) James I (b) Henry VIII (c) Charles II (d) George III

12

LOVE LIVES OF FAMOUS WOMEN

310. Which glamour girl was popularly known as 'Diamond Lil', the 'Screen's Bad Girl' and the 'Siren of Screen'?

(a) Mae West (b) Clara Bow (c) Anne Sheridan (d) Marilyn Monroe

311. Who made love with Baron Lepic in a hot-air balloon floating two hundred feet over the river Aude in France for more than an hour? Sixty years later, she remarked, 'It was an experience every woman should enjoy.'

(a) Adah Issacs Menken (b) Ninon de Lenclos (c) Kitty Fisher (d) La Belle Otero

312. One of her many lesbian lovers was Natalie Barney, an American expatriate in Paris. On one occasion, she sent Barney a message reading, "Natalie, my husband kisses your hands, and I the rest." Who was she?

(a) Eva Braun (b) Colette (c) Rosa Bonheur (d) Gertrude Stein

313. This woman in seventh century B.C. was variously depicted as "the tenth Muse" and a "marvel among women". Perhaps the most famous lesbian in history, who is she?

(a) Lesbia (b) Cecilia (c) Agrippina (d) Sappho

314. She met her lover Gilbert Roland during the filming of *The Plastic Age*. But when he proposed marriage, she dismissed the proposal saying that no man would ever win her. Who was she?

(a) Brigitte Bardot (b) Sophia Loren (c) Marlene Dietrich (d) Clara Bow

315. She was the wife of a Roman emperor. She had a room in the imperial palace where she forced ladies of the nobility to engage in intercourse with men of her choosing, sometimes while the woman's husband watched. Who was she?

(a) Cleopatra (b) Messalina (c) Julia (d) Agrippina

316. Which famous lady, lunching with her friends at the time of her husband's retirement, when asked what she was looking forward to in the years ahead, replied, 'A penis'?

(a) Madame de Gaulle (b) Mrs. Jimmy Carter (c) Mrs. Ronald Reagan (d) Josephine Baker

317. Which famous woman married the baseball star Joe DiMaggio and the playright Arthur Miller?

(a) Moll Flanders (b) Marilyn Monroe (c) Elizabeth Taylor (d) Sophia Loren

318. Which English courtesan became famous for her uninhibited *Memoirs* published in 1825, which became so successful that it sold thirty editions in a year?

(a) Kitty Fisher (b) La Belle Otero (c) Harriette Wilson (d) Adah Issacs Menken

13
SUPERLATIVES OF SEX

319. Where do you find the largest collection of sex books?

(a) The Vatican Library (b) The Kinsey Institute (c) Bibliotheque Nationale, Paris (d) National Library of Medicine, Bethesda

320. There are one hundred and ninety-three living species of monkeys and apes. Which of them is supposed to have the largest penis?

(a) Gorilla (b) Chimpanzee (c) Rhesus monkey (d) Man

321. When was the first ever human vaginal transplant done?

(a) 1960 (b) 1973 (c) 1987 (d) Never

322. Where was the first commercial sperm bank opened?

(a) Paris (b) Washington (c) New York (d) London

323. Where was the first sperm bank opened in India?

(a) Tiruchirapalli (b) Bombay (c) Calcutta (d) New Delhi

324. Which famous lady is supposed to have been involved in the longest session of love-making?

(a) Marilyn Monroe (b) Cleopatra (c) Mae West (d) Queen Hatshepsut

14

SEXUAL ABERRATIONS AND PERVERSIONS

325. What is the name given to a Japanese female prostitute proper?

(a) Geisha (b) Hokan (c) Geiko (d) Joro

326. In Japan what is a Maiko?

(a) A girl who is being trained to become a prostitute (b) A prostitute who has a husband as a pimp (c) A girl prostitute less than 15 years old (d) A male prostitute

327. What is an Okasan?

(a) A male prostitute (b) A pimp (c) A geisha house manageress (d) A prostitute who specializes in oral sex

328. What type of girls are the Haori?

(a) They roam naked on streets (b) They have very big busts (c) They have large buttocks (d) They remain fully clad and provide simple entertainment

329. What type of girls are the Korobi?

(a) Girls with big and lusty eyes (b) Girls who sell their bodies (c) Girls who sleep on the streets (d) Girls with abnormally large breasts

330. What is Zoophilia?

(a) A sexual penchant for animals (b) Inability to make love (c) Ability to make love more than three times in an hour (d) Distaste at the sight of animals mating

331. Many adolescents find delight in watching animals copulate. What is this perversion called?

(a) Animaliphilia (b) Mixoscopic zoophilia (c) Animal perversion (d) Zoophobia

332. What is the term for sexual activity between humans and animals?

(a) Bestiality (b) Zooscopy (c) Zoography (d) Zoopinia

333. In medieval time, there was a fear that copulation between humans and animals would produce

monstrous hybrids. What was the terrible penalty inflicted on the defaulter?

(a) He was burnt (b) The animal was burnt (c) Both of the above (d) He was hanged, drawn and quartered

334. The abnormal condition in which one derives erotic pleasure from seeing other people making love is called

(a) algolagnia (b) mixoscopia (c) kleptolagnia (d) iconolagny

335. Abnormal erotic pleasure from seeing other people's genitals or underclothes is called

(a) merophilous (b) titallagnia (c) tantalolagnia (d) scoptophilia

336. Homosexual desire and sexual activity between women is called

(a) Lesbianism (b) Onanism (c) Voyeurism (d) Exhibitionism

337. In ancient Greece, which of its islands was noted for its homosexual women?

(a) Crete (b) Corfu (c) Lesbos (d) Cyclades

338. Which lesbian organization was founded in San Francisco in 1955?

(a) Gay Women (b) The Daughters of Bilitis (c) Hungry Wolves (d) Play Girls

339. Which monthly magazine does the above organization publish?

(a) *Gay Newsletter* (b) *Happy Plays* (c) *The Ladder* (d) *The Gay Activist*

340. A group of disorders in which sexual arousal and satisfaction occurs from unusual objects, rituals or situations is called

(a) paraphilia (b) haemophilia (c) philiophilia (d) klismaphilia

341. A disorder in which a person derives sexual satisfaction from female undergarments and shoes, etc., is called

(a) transvestism (b) pedophilia (c) exhibitionism (d) fetishism

342. Cross-dressing by heterosexual males for sexual excitement is called

(a) transvestism (b) pedophilia (c) exhibitionism (d) urophilia

343. Engaging in sexual activity with children is called

(a) mysophilia (b) fomentism (c) pedophilia (d) urophilia

344. Exposing genitals to an unsuspecting stranger for the purpose of obtaining sexual excitement is called

(a) mysophilia (b) exhibitionism (c) scatolgia (d) necrophilia

345. Habitual looking at unsuspecting people, who are either naked or in the act of disrobing is called

(a) voyeurism (b) sexual masochism (c) sexual sadism (d) atypical paraphilia

346. Getting pleasure from being humiliated, bound, beaten or otherwise made to suffer for sexual arousal, is an abnormal condition which is called

(a) atypical paraphilia (b) sexual masochism (c) sexual sadism (d) coprophilia

347. What is the abnormal condition in which inflicting physical or psychological pain on another person is necessary in order to achieve sexual excitement?

(a) Sexual sadism (b) Klismaphilia (c) Necrophilia (d) Coprophilia

348. Sexual arousal by faeces is called

(a) synorgasmia (b) tachorgasmia (c) coprophilia (d) mysophilia

349. Sexual arousal by rubbing against the genitalia or body of another is called

(a) spanogyny (b) syndyasmian (c) osculation (d) frotteurism

350. Sexual arousal by the giving or receiving of enemas is called

(a) enemaphilia (b) klismaphilia (c) neolagnia (d) matutolagnia

351. Sexual arousal by filth is called

(a) mysophilia (b) shunamitism (c) pygmalionism (d) necrophilia

352. Abnormal sexual interest in dead bodies and sexual intercourse with them is called

(a) urophilia (b) hypnudism (c) necrophilia (d) scatolgia

353. A condition in which a person gets sexual excitement by eating the flesh of dead bodies is called

(a) necrolagnia (b) necrophagia (c) necrosis (d) pining

354. Sexual arousal by urine is called

(a) urophilia (b) urophagia (c) uromania (d) uraemia

355. What is tribadism?

(a) A three-partner sex act (b) Two-partners in sexual union while a third watches (c) An erotic arousal on seeing television (d) Lesbianism

356. Insatiable sexual desire in women is called

(a) sexomania (b) insatiability (c) nymphomania (d) coprolapsia

357. In eonism males find sexual pleasure in

(a) visiting prostitutes (b) wearing female garments (c) daydreaming about girls (d) taking girls to costly restaurants

358. There is a general term for the perversion of sexual instincts, which includes sexual gratification by fingering, fondling, licking, etc. What is it?

(a) Uranism (b) Agoramania (c) Ailuromania (d) Kleptolagnia

359. The Greek god Zeus carried this boy off in the form of an eagle, for intercourse. Who was this attractive boy?

(a) Castor (b) Pollux (c) Ganymede (d) Hercules

360. Which famous lesbian was known as 'the Amazon' because of Rémy de Gourmont's immortalization of her in his *Lettres à l'Amazone*?

(a) Rosa Bonheur (b) Sappho (c) Emily Dickinson (d) Natalie Barney

361. In which sexual perversion, a husband arranges for his wife to have another male partner, so that he can fantasise her in the role of a prostitute?

(a) Troilism (b) Prostitutemania (c) Uxolagnia (d) Uxorophilia

362. Some people can get an arousal only when they fondle a stranger who is asleep. What is this aberration known as?

(a) Narcophilia (b) Somnophilia (c) Sleepmania (d) Fondlephilia

363. A condition in which one gets sexual pleasure only with old partners is called

(a) kleptophilia (b) gerontophilia (c) narrotophilia (d) acrotomophilia

364. What is Clytemnestra complex?

(a) A woman's obsessive impulse to kill her husband in order to possess one of his male relatives (b) A strange complex in which one gets sexual pleasure only when one rapes his own wife (c) A complex in which a man gets pleasure by engaging his wife in masturbation (d) Getting sexual pleasure by looking at obscene books

365. What is narrotophilia?

(a) Sexual stimulation from seeing corpses (b) Having sex with dead animals (c) Sexual stimulation from reading erotic materials (d) Sexual stimulation from seeing naked statues

366. The odour of vaginal secretions has a stimulating effect on some men. What is this perversion known as?

(a) Olfactory eroticism (b) Secretory eroticism (c) Abnormal eroticism (d) *Erotica vagina secreta*

367. What is Coprolalia?

(a) Abnormal sexual pleasure derived by eating dung (b) Smearing dung and filth on one's body (c) Getting sexual pleasure by defecating in public (d) Getting sexual pleasure by making obscene telephone calls

368. A psychosexual disorder in which an individual prefers to achieve sexual gratification by listening to stories of sexual encounters of others or to sounds of others produced during intercourse, either live or recorded, is called

(a) ecstasy (b) ecouteurism (c) menoxenia (d) sexophilia

369. What is dishabillophobia?

(a) Fear of sexual intercourse (b) Fear of female genital organs (c) Fear of undressing in front of someone (d) Fear of kissing

370. What is dippoldism?

(a) Getting sexual excitement by connecting genitals to live poles through wires (b) Getting sexual gratification from beating children (c) Viewing obscene films (d) Using a dildo to achieve orgasm

371. What is gamahuche?

(a) Sucking female breasts (b) Sucking female buttocks (c) Pinching female buttocks surreptitiously (d) Stimulating female genitals by mouth

372. A couple was engaged in oral sex. In a fit of passion, the male blew air into the vagina, causing sudden death of his female partner. What must have happened to her?

(a) Electrical disturbance of heart since air is a bad conductor of electricity (b) Blowing of bacteria into the vagina (c) Air embolism (d) Inadvertent spillage of saliva in the vagina which acts as a poison there

373. A dangerous sexual technique that uses oxygen deprivation to heighten the sensations of masturbation is known as

(a) atrium vaginae (b) autoerotic asphyxia (c) atresia uteri (d) asphyxia neonatorum

374. Engaging in sexual activities while imagining oneself as a child is known as

(a) automysophobia (b) autoscophophilia (c) autopedophilia (d) pederasty

375. Sexual gratification from looking at one's own body, particularly the genital organs is called

(a) autoscopophilia (b) autovoyeurism (c) autosomophilia (d) egophilia

376. A strange and rare fear of being dirty or having an odour about oneself may inhibit an individual's enjoyment of sexual activity. What is this strange fear called?

(a) Lallophobia (b) Stangophobia (c) Echophobia (d) Automysophobia

377. Some individuals have a rare fear of any wind instrument, particularly the flute, because it has a resemblance to a phallus. What is this rare fear known as?

(a) Aleurophobia (b) Aulophobia (c) Ascritophobia (d) Mammaphobia

378. Erotophobia means fear of

(a) sexy women (b) buttocks (c) sexual love (d) breasts

379. Hephephilia is a form of sexual perversion in which gratification is obtained by contact with

(a) nose (b) nasal secretions (c) dirt and grease (d) soft smooth fabrics

380. What is *equus eroticus*?

(a) Sex with a horse (b) Sex with either a horse or a donkey (c) One sex partner riding the other's back (d) Three women having sex together

381. Sexual interest in statues is called

(a) pyromania (b) vampirism (c) coprophagia (d) pygmalionism

382. When acute sexual excitement is produced by the setting and the sight of large destructive fires, leading to urination, erection, masturbation and spontaneous orgasm at the scene, the aberration is called

(a) pyromania (b) pyrophagia (c) pyrophobia (d) urolagnia

383. Fear of female genitals is called

(a) maritophobia (b) gynaephobia (c) eurotophobia (d) klismaphobia

384. Medorthophobia is the fear of

(a) naked statues (b) erect penis (c) women's panties (d) going alone with a new date

385. Stimulation of the anus with the tongue is known as

(a) coprolalia (b) anilingus (c) lingus-e-ani (d) *stimulatio ani*

386. What are or were ben-wa?

(a) Whores who provide oral sex (b) Japanese girls who engage in erotic telephonic conversation for a small fee (c) A set of balls used by women for discreet masturbation (d) Leather whips to achieve sadistic pleasure

387. Which is the most widespread type of fetishism?

(a) Foot fetishism (b) Cloth fetishism (c) Handkerchief fetishism (d) Rubber fetishism

388. What is commonly referred to as 'Greek love'?

(a) Platonic love in which there is no sexual element at all (b) Oral sex (c) Self defilement by hand (d) Anal coitus

389. Which of the following statements is true about voyeurists?

(a) They are completely harmless (b) They usually rape the females they have seen naked (c) They start making obscene call to the female they have seen naked (d) They take nude photographs and start blackmailing the lady

390. What is presbyophilia?

(a) Sexual love for cats (b) Sexual love for the aged (c) An insane desire to have intercourse with a female elephant (d) A love for walking nude in the rain

391. What is spectrophilia?

(a) Love of rainbows (b) Desire to make love in the rain (c) Desire to make love in the day only (d) Sexual love for spirits

392. Who are osphresiolagniacs?

(a) People who can't make love (b) People who make love only to young girls (c) People who get stimulated by body odours (d) People who want to have intercourse with their neighbour's wives

393. What is nympholepsy?

(a) Infatuation with young girls (b) An insane desire to have intercourse with fairies (c) Dreaming of nude girls (d) A compulsion to buy nudie magazines

394. Erotographomania is

(a) compulsive desire to look at breasts (b) insane desire to touch breasts (c) insane desire to mutilate sexual parts of animals (d) compulsive desire to write on or draw sexual subjects

395. Many men and women in North Africa and Arabia specialize in *qerdz*. What is it?

(a) Fellatio (b) Erotic dancing (c) Buttock swaying (d) Wife swapping

396. Sexual intercourse by several men with one girl is known colloquially as

(a) Gang bang (b) Bang gang (c) Bingo gang (d) Rape gang

397. When can a husband be prosecuted for committing rape on his own wife?

(a) When the sexual act was done during the wife's sleep (b) When the act was done without her consent (c) When the wife is below 15 years of age (d) When the act is done in front of a third person

398. According to Indian law, what should be the minimum age of a girl, below which she cannot give valid consent for sexual intercourse?

(a) 10 years (b) 12 years (c) 16 years (d) 18 years

399. Rape by persons who are in position of authority, such as police officers, jail wardens and hospital staff is called

(a) gang rape (b) authoritarian rape (c) forced rape (d) custodial rape

400. If rape cannot be proved or there is any reasonable doubt as to the intent of rape, the accused may be convicted of the lesser offence of indecent assault on a female. Which section of the Indian Penal Code lays down punishment for such an offence?

(a) 312 (b) 320 (c) 354 (d) 377

401. If sexual arousal is caused by giving or receiving pain, the condition is called

(a) eesome (b) algolagnia (c) crurophilous (d) nomogamosis

402. The abnormal condition in which sexual arousal is caused by legs is called

(a) crurophilous (b) hyphephilia (c) kleptolagnia (d) punalua

403. The condition when sexual arousal is caused by caressing the breasts is called

(a) undinism (b) pygophilous (c) mazophilous (d) erotomastia

404. The condition when sexual arousal is caused by touching or rubbing the nipples of a female is called

(a) venust (b) cherophilia (c) thelerethism (d) desanimania

405. The condition when sexual arousal is caused by viewing erotic pictures is known as

(a) iconolagny (b) phrenophilia (c) cheromania (d) stupemania

406. The abnormal condition in which sexual arousal is caused by the sight of water is known as

(a) idiolagnia (b) undinism (c) cresophilia (d) timbrophilia

15

FAMOUS BOOKS AND MAGAZINES OF SEX

407. Bob Guccione is the founder and editor-publisher of which famous sex magazine?

(a) *Playboy* (b) *Playgirl* (c) *Men Only* (d) *Penthouse*

408. These are bawdy, sexy and humorous five-line poems. What are they called?

(a) Lampoon (b) Irony (c) Limerick (d) Occasional verse

409. Who is the compiler of the famous book called *The Limerick*?

(a) Mukul Sharma (b) Gershon Legman (c) Lupercalia (d) Edward Lear

410. In which year was the *Playboy* magazine founded?

(a) 1901 (b) 1921 (c) 1953 (d) 1964

411. Who was the founder of *Playboy* magazine?

(a) Hugh Marston Hefner (b) Charles Waterton (c) Briton Hadden (d) Henry Robinson Luce

412. Who wrote the bestselling book *Sexual Behaviour in the Human Male* in 1948?

(a) Dr. Basil Purdue (b) Alfred Kinsey (c) Anthony Busuttil (d) All of the three above jointly

413. Which famous glamour girl appeared on the cover of the first issue of *Playboy*?

(a) Kim Novak (b) Ursula Andress (c) Brigitte Bardot (d) Marilyn Monroe

414. Who was the 'Sweetheart of the month' in the first issue of *Playboy*?

(a) Kim Novak (b) Ursula Andress (c) Brigitte Bardot (d) Marilyn Monroe

415. What was the cost of the first issue of *Playboy*?

(a) 50 cents (b) 1 dollar (c) 2 dollars (d) 5 dollars

416. The first issue of *Playboy* was an immediate success. How many copies of that issue were sold?

(a) Between 10,000 and 20,000 copies (b) Between 50,000 and 60,000 copies (c) Between 80,000 and 90,000 copies (d) More than 100,000 copies

417. Whom did Hefner choose as editor of *Playboy* for its inaugural issue?

(a) Ray Russel (b) Art Paul (c) George Paul (d) Dr. Iain West

418. Probably the most important symbol associated with *Playboy* is its rabbit. Who designed it?

(a) Ray Russel (b) Art Paul (c) George Paul (d) Dr Iain West

419. For the inaugural issue of *Playboy*, Hefner bought a series of nudes of Marilyn Monroe from a Chicago calendar company. How much did he pay the company.?

(a) $100 (b) $500 (c) $1000 (d) $5000

420. How much did Hefner pay Marilyn Monroe to get her permission to print her nudes in the magazine?

(a) $ 500 (b) $ 5,000 (c) $ 50,000 (d) Her permission was not taken at all

421. In which year did the circulation of *Playboy* hit the astounding 800,000 mark?

(a) 1954 (b) 1956 (c) 1962 (d) 1965

422. In the above year, *Playboy* became the most widely-read men's magazine. Which magazine had occupied this exalted position before?

(a) *Men Only* (b) *Playgirl* (c) *Penthouse* (d) *Esquire*

423. In 1963, Hefner fought the courts over the printing of a picture showing a glamour girl lying in bed revealing a naked breast. Who was this glamour girl?

(a) Bo Derek (b) Tallulah Bankhead (c) Jayne Mansfield (d) Ursula Andress

424. What was the outcome of the above case?

(a) Hefner won (b) Hefner lost and paid $ 10,000 (c) Hefner lost but did not pay anything, resulting in a closure of magazine for 2 years (d) Hefner bribed the judge to close the case

425. In 1959, a tragedy befell Hefner mainly because of his dedication to *Playboy*. What happened?

(a) He made two of his models pregnant (b) His wife divorced him (c) He broke leg while going to a photo session for *Playboy* (d) One of his photographers sued him for $ 1,000,000 and won.

426. How many copies of *Playboy* were selling per month in 1964?

(a) 1 million (b) 2 million (c) 5 million (d) 10 million

427. How many copies of *Playboy* were selling per month in 1968?

(a) 5 million (b) 10 million (c) 15 million (d) 20 million

428. How many copies of *Playboy* were selling per month in 1972?

(a) 7 million (b) 10 million (c) 15 million (d) 20 million

429. In the 1960s Hefner was travelling the world in his private jet. What was it called?

(a) *Playboy* (b) *Big Bunny* (c) *Sweetheart* (d) *Angel Tits*

430. Who published *Pornography and the Law* in 1960 and *Sex Histories of American College Men* and *Sexual Response in Women* in 1964?

(a) William H. Masters (b) Virginia Johnson (c) Phyllis Kronhausen (d) Eberhard Kronhausen

431. Who is 1832 wrote and published *The Fruits of Philosophy,* one of the first books on contraceptive techniques?

(a) Richard von Krafft-Ebing (b) Lily Langtry (c) David Herbert Lawrence (d) Charles Knowlton

432. Which famous psychologist wrote *Three Contributions to the Sexual Theory* in 1905?

(a) Alfred Adler (b) Sigmund Freud (c) Karen Horney (d) Raymond Cattell

433. Who wrote *Sexual Behaviour in the Human Female* in 1953?

(a) Anthony Busuttil (b) Bernard Knight (c) Alfred Kinsey (d) William H. Masters

434. Who wrote the bestselling book *Patterns of Sexual Behaviour* in 1951?

(a) C.S. Ford (b) F.A. Beach (c) Sigmund Freud (d) Alfred Kinsey

435. Which famous person wrote *Human Sexual Response* in 1966?

(a) Havelock Ellis (b) William H. Masters (c) Helen Kaplan (d) Virginia E. Johnson

436. Who wrote the bestseller *Human Sexual Inadequacy* in 1970?

(a) Havelock Ellis (b) William H. Masters (c) Helen Kaplan (d) Virginia E. Johnson

437. Who wrote *The Joy of Sex* in 1972?

(a) Alex Comfort (b) Alfred C. Kinsey (c) T.H. Van De Velde (d) Helen Kaplan

438. Who wrote *The New Sex Therapy* in 1974?

(a) Ellen Craft (b) Helen Kaplan (c) Barbara Ann Malpass (d) None of the above

439. Who wrote the well-known Hindu treatise on sex, *Kama Sutra*?

(a) Charak (b) Vagabhatta (c) Susruta (d) Mallanaga

440. When was *Kama Sutra* written?

(a) Before 4000 B.C. (b) Between 4000 B.C. and 3000 B.C. (c) Between 1000 B.C. and 500 B.C. (d) Between A.D. 100 and 400

441. Who first translated *Kama Sutra* in English?

(a) Aldous Huxley (b) Sir Richard Burton (c) David Attenborough (d) Sigmund Freud

442. This bestselling sex manual written in 1926 was banned by Vatican city and also by Hitler, for reasons unknown. Which was this sex manual?

(a) English translation of *Kama Sutra* (b) *Joy of Sex* (c) *Pleasures of Oral Sex* (d) *Ideal Marriage*

443. Which famous magazine devoted its entire September 1969 issue to the erotic engravings of Picasso?

(a) *Avant-Garde* (b) *Time* (c) *New Yorker* (d) *Playboy*

444. Which famous person reputedly destroyed 160 tons of erotic books, magazines and pictures in his drive against immorality?

(a) Morarji Desai (b) Adolf Hitler (c) Anthony Comstock (d) Ronald Reagan

445. How many different kinds of love-bites are described in *Kama Sutra*?

(a) 8 (b) 64 (c) 128 (d) 1056

446. Which illustrated fifteenth century sex manual from India includes specific physiological advice on marital and sexual satisfaction, and positions for lovemaking?

(a) *Kama Sutra* (b) *Koka Shastra* (c) *Ananda Marga* (d) *Ananga Ranga*

447. Which book led to the passing of the first Obscene Publications Act in 1857 in England?

(a) *The School of Venus* (b) *Fanny Hill* (c) *Juliette* (d) All the above books

448. His *Sonetti Lussuriosi* (1524) was a collection of verses and erotic drawings that demonstrated positions for sexual intercourse. The book was extremely popular and got him into trouble with the Pope. Who was he?

(a) Edward Adrizzone (b) Pietro Aretino (c) Alfred Domett (d) Ernulphus

449. Who wrote the bestseller *Everything You Always Wanted to Know about Sex but Were Afraid to Ask*?

(a) Eric Berne (b) Dr. Benjamin Spock (c) David Reuben (d) Issac Asimov

450. What are or were the pillow books?

(a) Chinese sex manuals illustrating the various positions for intercourse (b) Erotic books meant for bachelors primarily (c) Leaflets distributed by Soho prostitutes by hand (d) A weekly directory published by French prostitutes giving a list of their addresses and fees

451. In which year was the girlie magazine *Penthouse* started?

(a) 1953 (b) 1961 (c) 1965 (d) 1972

452. *Esquire* was one of the first magazines offering pin-ups for the sophisticated male. In which year did it start offering pin-ups?

(a) 1901 (b) 1911 (c) 1921 (d) 1933

453. Gradually *Esquire* lost interest in pin-ups and finally abandoned the practice altogether. In which issue did the last pin-up appear?

(a) January 1950 (b) March 1953 (c) October 1958 (d) December 1965

454. Which was the first high-class men's magazine to show pubic hair?

(a) *Playboy* (b) *Penthouse* (c) *Men Only* (d) *Esquire*

455. Who was the first girl bold enough to expose pubic hair for a pin-up photograph?

(a) Marilyn Monroe (b) Stephanie McLean (c) Clara Harrow (d) Jeanette Wilson

456. How many coital positions are described in the Indian sex manual *Ananga Ranga*?

(a) 32 (b) 64 (c) 1,028 (d) 10,056

457. How many coital positions are described in the Islamic sex manual *The Perfumed Garden*?

(a) 1 only (b) 2 (c) 10 (d) 40

458. Who were the authors of the bestselling books *ABZ of Love* and *XYZ of Love*?

(a) Masters and Johnson (b) Inge and Sten Hegeler (c) Phyllis and Eberhard Kronhausen (d) Sigmund Freud and Karen Horney

459. Who wrote *Love in Action* (1959), a cross-cultural study of sexual behaviour?

(a) Riddley Walker (b) Russel Hoban (c) Fernando Henriques (d) Brian Aldiss

460. According to which Taoist sex manual, written around the birth of Christ, was it possible to judge a woman's sexual features by scrutinising her face?

(a) *Yu Mi Chueh* (b) *Hoshiwara Kau* (c) *Li po tao* (d) *Xan Li*

461. How many coital positions are described in the bestselling sex manual *Ideal Marriage*?

(a) 2 (b) 10 (c) 500 (d) 1000

462. Who is the author of the bestselling book *The Female Eunuch*?

(a) Alex Comfort (b) Eric Berne (c) Kate Webster (d) Germaine Greer

463. Which American sex newspaper, founded in 1968, is published weekly by Milky Way Productions?

(a) *Screw* (b) *Hustler* (c) *Men Only* (d) *Orgasm*

464. This English pornographer served in the Indian army for several years and became a Hindu scholar. His motto for life was *Vivat Lingam, Non Resurgam* (Long live erection, there will be no resurrection). He wrote a flagellation epic *The Adventures of Lady Lovesport and the Audacious Harry*, which is considered a porn classic. Who is he?

(a) Sir Charles Sedley (b) Edward Sellon (c) Al Goldstein (d) Felicien Rops

465. The *Kama Sutra* devotes a whole chapter entitled *auparishtaka* to this activity. What is it?

(a) Anal congress (b) Masturbation (c) Fellatio (d) Cunnilingus

16
STRANGE CUSTOMS

466. What is a Malay kiss?

(a) Two people rubbing their noses (b) A kiss between two men (c) A kiss between two women (d) Two people kissing with their arms entwined around each other's waist

467. In medieval Europe, women having extra breasts were considered as

(a) goddesses (b) witches (c) sexually very satisfying (d) sexually unsatisfying

468. Which group of people, deliberately elongate the labia minora by pulling them or hanging weights from them?

(a) Bhils (b) Santhals (c) Ponape of the Caroline Islands (d) Kalahari Bushmen

469. What is a Hottentot apron?

(a) An apron worn by doctors while performing deliveries (b) An apron worn by the couple during sexual activity (c) Artificially enlarged and elongated labia (d) A flower whose smell stimulates sexual desire.

470. What is a French kiss?

(a) A kiss that is blown in air (b) A kiss that is taken by deception (c) A kiss between a brother and a sister (d) A kiss in which each partner's tongue explores the other's mouth

471. What is a *maraichinage*?

(a) A French kiss that lasts for several hours (b) A violent sexual union (c) A kiss in which each partner draws blood from the other's lips (d) A French delicacy eaten just before love-making to increase sexual powers

472. Which of the following societies considers kissing a disgusting practice?

(a) Balinese (b) Fijians (c) Greenlanders (d) Russians

473. What is the Nasamonian custom?

(a) A strange custom in which newly married couple kiss each other's nose (b) A custom whereby a newly married bride has to perform a nude dance before the guests (c) A primitive marriage custom in which all the wedding guests copulate with the bride (d) A custom where the bridegroom has the right to copulate with his bride's mother.

474. What is a tree marriage?

(a) A marriage performed under a tree (b) A marriage in which the bride or groom marries a tree

(c) A marriage in which each marriage guest plants a sapling to enrich the environment (d) A marriage in which the bride and the bridegroom are asked to cut a tree before they can go to bed.

475. In ancient Sparta, a husband sometimes loaned his wife to a more vigorous man, in order to ensure the superiority of Spartan children. Who is said to have advocated this custom?

(a) Lycurgus (b) Alexander the Great (c) Sophocles (d) Aristophanes

476. To assure a plentiful harvest, what did a farmer in ancient Rome do at the beginning of the planting season?

(a) Flog his naked wife to appease the gods (b) Sacrifice a virgin girl at the altar of the gods (c) Ritually urinate on the field to ensure plentiful rain (d) Went out to the fields and ritually copulated with his wife

477. According to Roman law, if a virgin was to be executed in ancient Rome for some crime, a curious act was first performed. What was it?

(a) She was paraded naked on the streets of Rome (b) She was first flogged at a market place (c) She had to perform fellatio on the Roman king (d) She was ceremonially deflowered

478. In which of the following books, *Vish Kanyas* or poison damsels are sent as dancing girls to enemy countries to do damages?

(a) *Harsha Charita* (b) *Akbarnamah* (c) *Garuda Purana* (d) *Katha Sarit Sagara*

479. In the *Mudra Rakshasha* of Visakhadatta, written about the seventh century A.D., someone sends a Vishkanya to King Chandragupta, but he is saved by his minister Chanakya who passes the girl on to another king who succumbs to her fatal love. Who was that unfortunate king?

(a) Vasavadatta (b) Parvataka (c) Harsha (d) Kaushambi

480. Some primitive societies follow a strange custom called Couvade. What is this custom?

(a) The father takes to bed before and during the delivery of a child (b) Man having intercourse with wife just before delivery to inject 'extra life' into the child. (c) Two brothers marrying their own sister, so that she doesn't go out of the family (d) Father marrying his widowed daughters to look after their social security

481. What is night courting?

(a) Sexual intercourse at night (b) Going out to look for girls in the night (c) Man and woman sharing the same bed but not engaging in sexual intercourse (d) Making love more than seven times in a single night

482. This is a state of great excitement often found among Malay women, and is accompanied by hallucinations of a sexual content. Name this condition.

(a) Latah (b) Librium (c) Extratemporal perception (d) Etherial state

483. The strange custom of cutting off of female breasts was prevalent in

(a) Ancient Greece (b) Ancient Ireland (c) Ancient India (d) All the above places

484. These ancient people were in the habit of having their drinking cups modelled after the shapes of the breasts of their sweethearts or mistresses and went to the extent of making actual casts of their breasts. Who were these ancient lovers?

(a) Aztecs (b) Romans (c) Egyptians (d) Akkadians

485. Among some Arabian tribes, a man who is pursued in blood-feud and closely pressed by his enemies, will often take refuge in a strange tent or camp and do something to ensure that he is protected. What is this act?

(a) Make love to one of the females of the house (b) Show them his sword (c) Give them a costly gift (d) Kiss the bare breast of a woman

486. In ancient Egyptian hieroglyphics, the signatures of kings, queens, etc. were enclosed in a panel-like figure, called a Cartouche. How did the signatures of queens differ from those of kings?

(a) They were enclosed in a curious shape resembling the vulva (b) They were anointed with costly perfumes (c) They were followed by the representation of an egg and profile of a breast (d) Female pubic hair were stuck on those signatures

487. According to astrology, which constellation of stars govern the sexual organs?

(a) Scorpio (b) Libra (c) Aquarius (d) Pisces

488. According to astrology which planet controls the womb and the testicles?

(a) Jupiter (b) Saturn (c) Venus (d) Neptune

489. In ancient Rome, there were some very beautiful women who went about naked habitually. What were they called?

(a) Hetaerae (b) Doris (c) Lupae (d) Fornices

490. What is the practice of infibulation?

(a) Removing the fibula bone of a young girl to make her legs look more delicate (b) Beating a couple with a whip just after marriage to ensure their fertility (c) Examining the garments of a newly married bride for spots of blood (d) Ensuring chastity by interfering with the genitals

491. In which Algerian desert tribe do the girls leave their settlements at the age of twelve and earn their dowries by dancing and prostitution?

(a) Ouled Nail (b) Semites (c) Hopi (d) Tazika

492. What is streaking?

(a) Having sexual intercourse at public places such as beaches (b) Throwing stones at copulating animals (c) Running naked on streets or public places (d) Soliciting customers for prostitution in broad daylight.

493. Some Arab bathhouses have special attendants called *bellaneh* who offer a special service to their customers. What do they do?

(a) Rub one's naked body with soap (b) Lick one's body clean (c) Provide sensual massage (d) Shave pubic hair

494. In this ancient society, a man whose wife was infertile or unattractive could ask another man, whose wife

was fecund, to let him have intercourse with her so that she could bear him a child. Adultery was thus technically unknown. Which was this society?

(a) Spartans (b) Harappans (c) Akkadians (d) Aztecs

495. What is the name given to the custom of allowing a girl to sleep with her fiancé, so that they can see how well they get on in bed together?

(a) Dating (b) Fondling (c) Bundling (d) Distancing

496. These ancient people auctioned off marriageable girls every year. Men had to bid high for the most attractive girls and this money was used as dowry to accompany ugly girls, whom nobody would otherwise buy. Who were these ancient people?

(a) Harappans (b) Mayans (c) Aztecs (d) Babylonians

497. Which god is supposed to have married his own sister, while still in the womb?

(a) Osiris (b) Peleus (c) Orpheus (d) Quetzalcoatl

498. On which ancient Roman fertility god's erect phallus was a new bride required to sit before joining her husband in bed?

(a) Priapus (b) Centaur (c) Janus (d) Mutunus Tutunus

499. What is or was a levirate marriage?

(a) Marriage of a woman with her stepson (b) Inadvertent marriage between a brother and a sister (c) Marriage of a widow to her brother-in-law (d) A tradition in ancient Sparta, whereby a rapist had to marry the girl he raped and had to look after her financially

500. What is a cluster marriage?

(a) A marriage in which a girl marries a cluster of trees (b) Young children playfully marrying one another (c) Marriage within the members of same family (d) Marriage in which two or three married couples live together and share spouses

501. What is adelphogamy?

(a) Marriage with a beast (b) Marriage with a female statue (c) Marriage in which brothers have a common wife (d) Marriage in which two friends marry each other's sister

502. According to ancient Roman law, what was confarreation?

(a) Taking a vow never to marry (b) Practice of catching female prisoners of war and marrying them (c) Giving capital punishment to anyone who indulge in oral sex (d) Marriage in which the husband had absolute legal control over his wife

503. What is dysonogamia?

(a) A second legal marriage (b) Marriage between persons of markedly different ages (c) Marriage between persons of markedly different social strata (d) Marriage with a foreigner

504. Marriage within one's tribe or group is called

(a) endogamy (b) exogamy (c) digamy (d) heterogamy

505. Marriage with someone of markedly lower social position is called

(a) heterogamosis (b) homogamosis (c) mésalliance (d) isonogamia

506. In some communities a custom exists whereby the man marries his wife's sister after the wife dies. What is this marriage called?

(a) Sororate (b) Punalua (c) Isonogamia (d) Digamy

507. What is traditionally given to a Chinese bridegroom on the day of his marriage, as a token of the wish that his wife may prove fruitful?

(a) A cup of herbal tea made from local aphrodisiac plants (b) Two eggs (c) A red thread to tie on his virgin bride's hair (d) A glass of warm milk with cardamom in it

508. What are the Tobias nights?

(a) Nights when a woman is menstruating (b) Nights when women were driven out of the house, so strangers could fornicate with them (c) Moonless nights during honeymoon (d) Three nights of sexual abstinence between marriage and consummation

509. What was the notorious custom of *droit de Seigneur* which was prevalent in France before the eighteenth century?

(a) The king could order any girl to strip (b) The boy's parents had to give dowry to the girl's (c) The king had the right of first sexual intercourse with any girl (d) The marching of all prostitutes on city streets with their faces blackened

510. In ancient and medieval Japan, a strange custom of *Tchin-chan* was followed. What was it?

(a) Showing the naked bride to all marriage guests (b) Asking all marriage guests to copulate with the bride (c) Bridegroom asking two nubile virgins as a dowry (d) Local priest demanding the right of first sexual intercourse from every nubile girl.

17

SEX SCANDALS

511. With whom did Devika Rani elope?

(a) Najmul Hassan (b) Himanshu Rai (c) Guru Dutt (d) K.L. Saigal

512. One of the most famous sex scandals in British history involved the Cabinet minister Cecil Parkinson. In whose ministry was he a member?

(a) Sir Winston Churchill (b) Harold Macmillan (c) Harold Wilson (d) Mrs. Margaret Thatcher

513. Which British call-girl was at the centre of the Profumo scandal of 1963?

(a) Bo Derek (b) Mandy Rice Devis (c) Christine Keeler (d) Pamella Bordes

514. Which portfolio did John Profumo hold when he was involved in the sex scandal mentioned above?

(a) Secretary of State for War (b) Finance Secretary (c) Home Minister (d) Agriculture and Industry Minister

515. On 22 March 1963, Profumo made a celebrated statement to the House of Commons. What was this statement?

(a) That he had sex with Christine Keeler (b) That he had sold war secrets to Russia (c) That Christine

Keeler was actually his cousin (d) That he never had sexual relations with Christine Keeler

516. In the sex scandal of Profumo, one person committed suicide in the end. Who was he/she?

(a) Dr. Stephen Ward (b) Christine Keeler (c) John Profumo (d) John Profumo's wife

517. Léonie d'Aunet, a young noblewoman, was one of the mistresses of this famous person. When their affair turned into a shocking sex scandal, Léonie's husband arranged to have the couple tailed by the police, who caught them red-handed. Although this famous person escaped punishment using his influence, Léonie was jailed for adultery. Who was this famous person?

(a) Benjamin Disraeli (b) William Gladstone (c) Victor Hugo (d) Charlie Chaplin

518. Jean Armour was one of the most beautiful women in his life. In February 1786 when she became pregnant they signed a document declaring each other as man and wife but Jean's father got a lawyer to destroy the signed document because the boy was very poor. Who was he?

(a) Robert Burns (b) Père Alexandre Dumas (c) Franz Josef Haydn (d) Edward Jenner

519. With which famous *Playboy* model was Steffi's father Peter Graf supposed to have an illicit relationship?

(a) Laura Temple (b) Mary Weisse (c) Nicole Meissner (d) Clara Kirkpatrick

520. With which woman was the famous tennis player Martina Navratilova supposed to have lesbian relationships?

(a) Virginia Wade (b) Judy Nelson (c) Maureen Connolly (d) Beth Underwood

521. At this spot a beautiful young daughter of a top British official, member of the Viceroy's household, eloped with a dashing young Indian prince. So infamous did this scandal become that this spot is still known as the Scandal Point. In which hill resort would you find this spot?

(a) Nainital (b) Darjeeling (c) Simla (d) Interlaaken

522. Which US president sent General Charles C. Pinckney to Britain to select four pretty girls as mistresses — two for the general and two for himself, creating a minor sex scandal?

(a) George Washington (b) John Adams (c) Thomas Jefferson (d) James Madison

523. Gossip was rife in Rome about his sexual appetites and the streets resounded with ribald songs about him. His family traced a legendary decent from Venus and Aeneas. Who was he?

(a) Augustus (b) Tiberius (c) Caligula (d) Julius Caesar

524. When this famous actress sued her private secretary Daisy DeVoe for embezzling $16,000, DeVoe retaliated by making her mistress's sexual escapades public. Who was this famous actress?

(a) Mae West (b) Greta Garbo (c) Brigitte Bardot (d) Clara Bow

525. Who brought a charge of sexual harassment against Clarence Thomas, just before he was to be confirmed as a judge of the US Supreme Court, erupting a major sex scandal of the 1990s?

(a) Anita Hill (b) Susann Myrrh (c) Dela Fayworth (d) Shiela Garvie

526. Born in Arezzo, Tuscany in 1492, this Italian pornographer, poet, and satirist reputedly attacked and blackmailed Michelangelo for his homosexuality. Who was he?

(a) Francesco Petrarca (b) Pietro Aretino (c) Theophile Gautier (d) Ludovico Ariosto

527. Which famous Hollywood film star was alleged to have inserted a Coke bottle into the vagina of starlet Virginia Rappe, causing her to bleed and die?

(a) Roscoe 'Fatty' Arbuckle (b) Errol Flynn (c) Gary Cooper (d) Johny Weissmuller

18

SEX KILLINGS

528. This 11-year-old girl was reported missing from her Notting Hill home on 14 December 1931. Two days later her raped and strangled body was found lying in shrubs. Despite strong circumstantial evidence against a 41-year-old married laundry worker, Percy Orlando Rush, he couldn't be prosecuted. Who was this unfortunate girl?

(a) Vera Page (b) Kate Webster (c) Belle Gunness (d) Maria Groesbeek

529. This 8-year-old girl was found murdered in Florida on 12 April 1969. She had been stabbed, disembowelled and slashed in the genital region. Her killer, 29-year-old Kenneth Ray Wright, was apprehended after his fingerprints were found on one of the razor blades found on the scene of crime. Who was this girl?

(a) Christina Gilmour (b) Sheila Garvie (c) Camellia Jo Hand (d) Christiana Edmunds

530. This man-woman team of murderers, photographed a ten-year-old girl in obscene poses with their male member, tape recorded her screams under torture, killed her and buried her on the nearly Yorkshire Moors. Who were these dreadful killers?

(a) Jeannie Donald and H.H. Holmes (b) Alice Crimmins and Alfred John Monson (c) Edith Carew and Charles Whitman (d) Myra Hindley and Ian Brady

531. This sexual criminal invited women to his house, got them drunk and then strangled and raped them, murdering at least six women in this way, including his own wife. In his teens he was sexually so inadequate that he was known as "Reggie-no-dick". Who was he?

(a) Chung Yi Miao (b) John Christie (c) George Chapman (d) Ronald Chesney

532. This 28-year-old wartime airman is frequently compared with Jack the Ripper on account of the

sexual mutilations he inflicted on his victims. Who was he?

(a) Gordon Frederick Cummins (b) Charles Howard Schmid (c) Robinson Hill (d) Arthur Devereux

533. When this sexual criminal was electrocuted at Sing Sing Prison on 16 January 1936, the first electrical charge failed because it was short-circuited by 29 metallic needles he had inserted in his genitals. Who was this queer criminal?

(a) Francis Flossie Forsyth (b) James Canham Read (c) Richard Robles (d) Albert Fish

534. He raped and murdered a four-year-old girl on 14 May 1948 and to apprehend him the police had to fingerprint the whole town of Blackburn. Who was he?

(a) Marcus Marymont (b) Peter Griffiths (c) David Greenwood (d) Styllon Christofi

535. Which American sex killer is known as the 'Gorilla Murderer'?

(a) Kenneth Neu (b) Michael Queripel (c) Earle Leonard Nelson (d) William Burke Kirwan

536. This psychopath found sexual gratification in burglary and murder. Once after killing a woman, he scrawled a message in lipstick on a wall, 'for heavens sake catch me before I kill more. I cannot control myself.' Who was he?

(a) Herbert John Bennett (b) Dean Corll (c) William Henry King (d) William Heirens

537. Which sex-killer was also known as the 'Beast of the Black Forest'?

(a) Heinrich Pommerencke (b) Reginald Ivor Hinks (c) Philip Cross (d) Albert T. Patrick

538. His nine murders accompanied by sexual assault earned him the nickname of "Sex Beast". Who was he?

(a) Ernest Brown (b) Derek Bentley (c) David Melvin Rees (d) Herbert Rowse Armstrong

539. He was a teetotaller and non-smoker with an insatiable sex-drive, who raped and killed thirteen women within

the space of only eighteen months. He was widely known as the Boston Strangler. Who was he?

(a) Wayne Boder (b) Albert Henry DeSalvo (c) Manfred Truber (d) Thomas Ross Young

540. This Canadian who became widely known as the Vampire Rapist had a sadistic obsession about breasts. From 1968 onwards he raped and killed at least five young women within a span of three years. He was ultimately caught when a dental expert demonstrated twenty-nine points of similarity between his teeth and the bite marks he had made on the breasts of one of his victims. Name him?

(a) Wayne Boden (b) John Hill (c) Georgi Markou (d) Manfred Truber

19

SEXUAL ACTIVITIES IN ANIMALS

541. What is the length of a stallion's penis?

(a) 6 inches (b) 12 inches (c) 18 inches (d) 2 1/2 feet

542. What is the length of a bull's penis?

(a) 12 inches (b) 18 inches (c) 24 inches (d) 30 inches

543. What is the length of an elephant's penis?

(a) 2 feet (b) 5 feet (c) 8 feet (d) 12 feet

544. A castrated animal, especially a horse, is known as a

(a) mettle (b) husker (c) corpse (d) gelding

545. How does a female camel behave just after the sexual intercourse is over?

(a) She attacks the male with her teeth (b) She licks the male (c) She totters away to search another male (d) She goes to sleep

546. What is the name given to the time when a female animal is in heat?

(a) Calorius (b) Dolorius (c) Estrus (d) Ovulatus

547. In which of the following animals do the testes lie in the abdomen?

(a) Elephants (b) Sloths (c) Fish (d) All of the above

548. In which of the following animals do the testes lie in scrotum during the breeding season, but remain within the abdomen during the non-breeding season?
(a) Insectivores (b) Bats (c) Rodents (d) All of the above

549. Gestation period is the period from the fertilization of an egg to the birth of the baby. What is the gestation period of a Golden Hamster?
(a) 16 days (b) 32 days (c) 64 days (d) 80 days

550. What is the gestation period of a laboratory mouse?
(a) 7 days (b) 19 days (c) 33 days (d) 45 days

551. What is the gestation period of a rat?
(a) 3 days (b) 7 days (c) 10 days (d) 22 days

552. What is the gestation period of a rabbit?
(a) 23 days (b) 31 days (c) 43 days (d) 53 days

553. What is the gestation period of a hedgehog?
(a) 35 days (b) 43 days (c) 57 days (d) 75 days

554. What is the gestation period of a polecat?
(a) 30 days (b) 40 days (c) 50 days (d) 60 days

555. What is the gestation period of an African elephant?
(a) 480 days (b) 640 days (c) 240 days (d) 360 days

556. Which of the following birds has the shortest gestation period?
(a) Song thrush (b) Nightingale (c) Lark (d) Blackbird

557. Which animal has the longest gestation period?
(a) Alpine Salamander (b) Blue Whale (c) Asiatic elephant (d) Hippopotamus

20
QUOTABLE QUOTES

558. This famous writer of sensuous literature opposed the theory that such type of literature could deprave or corrupt readers. He is known for his famous remark, 'Books copy behaviour, behaviour is not copied from books.' Who is he?

(a) Daniel Defoe (b) Theophile Gautier (c) Marcus Perennius (d) Petronius Arbiter

559. Who in 1855 saw a lady-in-waiting trip over at a state reception in Paris and remarked to the French empress, "I am delighted to see, Madame, that your ladies do not wear drawers and that the gates of paradise are always open"?

(a) King Victor Emmanuel of Sardinia (b) Queen Victoria (c) Prince Albert (d) Calvin Coolidge

560. Which famous person said, 'In German, a young lady has no sex, but a turnip has.'?

(a) Albert Einstein (b) Groucho Marx (c) Aldous Huxley (d) Mark Twain

561. Who said, 'Virginity is nothing but a big issue over a small tissue'?

(a) Brooke Shields (b) Sri Devi (c) Pooja Bedi (d) Greta Garbo

562. Who said, 'Sex is the central problem of life'?

(a) Havelock Ellis (b) Marie Stopes (c) Dr. Christian Barnard (d) Sigmund Freud

563. Who wrote to Jawaharlal Nehru, 'I think, I am not interested in sex as sex. There must be so much more to it, beauty of spirit and form. But I think you and I are in a minority'?

(a) Mahatma Gandhi (b) Sarojini Naidu (c) Lady Edwina Mountbatten (d) Isadora Duncan

564. Who said, 'I do all of my best work in bed'?

(a) Clara Bow (b) Marlene Dietrich (c) Jane Russell (d) Mae West

565. Who said, 'I've been in Who's Who and I know what's what, but it's the first time I ever made the dictionary'?

(a) Mae West (b) Clara Bow (c) Tallulah Bankhead (d) Jane Russell

566. Which noted painter is reputed to have said, 'Art is never chaste'?

(a) Georges Braque (b) Pablo Picasso (c) Peter Paul Rubens (d) Rembrandt

567. Who could have written 'a pretty girl who naked is/is worth a million statues'?

(a) W.H. Auden (b) Lord Byron (c) William Carloz Williams (d) E.E. Cummings

568. Which famous Greek said, "Marriage is a necessary evil"?

(a) Socrates (b) Euripides (c) Menander (d) Thucydides

569. Which famous actress said, 'Give a man a free hand and he'll run it all over you'?

(a) Clara Bow (b) Mae West (c) Jane Russel (d) Marlene Dietrich

570. Who said, 'Sex is one of the nine reasons for re-incarnation... The other eight are unimportant.'?

(a) Henry Miller (b) George Orwell (c) Mark Twain (d) D.H. Lawrence

571. Who said, 'Sex, treated properly, can be one of the most gorgeous things in the world'?

(a) Lillian Hellman (b) Elizabeth Taylor (c) Norman Mailer (d) D.H. Lawrence

572. Who said, 'People kill each other in bed. Some of the greatest crimes ever committed were committed in bed. And no weapons were used'?

(a) Aga Khan III (b) M.K. Gandhi (c) Nancy Astor (d) Norman Mailer

573. Who said, 'Familiarity breeds contempt — and children'?

(a) Franz Kafka (b) Oliver Wendell Holmes (c) Mark Twain (d) Oscar Wilde

574. Who is supposed to have said, 'Only good girls keep diaries. Bad girls don't have the time'?

(a) Tallulah Bankhead (b) Clara Bow (c) Zeenat Aman (d) Marilyn Monroe

575. Who is supposed to have exclaimed, 'All this fuss about sleeping together. For physical pleasure I'd sooner go to my dentist any day'?

(a) Evelyn Waugh (b) Lady Diana Cooper (c) Lord Chesterfield (d) George Bernard Shaw

576. Who said, 'women are a decorative sex. They never have anything to say, but they say it charmingly'?

(a) Petronius (b) Oscar Wilde (c) Ambrose Bierce (d) Lady Mary Wortley Montagu

577. Who said, 'Love is only the dirty trick played on us to achieve continuation of the species'?

(a) Alfred Hitchcock (b) John Ford (c) Samuel Johnson (d) W. Somerset Maugham

578. 'Sex is bad for one. But its' good for two.' Who made this famous remark?

(a) Woody Allen (b) Johnny Walker (c) Groucho Marx (d) Tuntun

579. Who said, 'What men desire is a virgin who is a whore'?

(a) Thomas Fuller (b) Amitabh Bachchan (c) Edward Dahlberg (d) Charles Roupell

580. Who is supposed to have remarked, 'At certain times I like sex — like after a cigarette'?

(a) Rodney Dangerfield (b) Jonathan Swift (c) Voltaire (d) Dorothy Parker

581. Who exclaimed, 'Is sex dirty? Only when it is being done right'?

(a) Rousseau (b) Woody Allen (c) Oscar Wilde (d) Thomas Fuller

582. Who said, 'What happens is that, as with drugs, one needs a stronger shot each time, and women are just women. The consumption of one woman is the consumption of all. You can't double the dose'?

(a) Ian Fleming (b) Gore Vidal (c) Disraeli (d) Juvenal

583. Who remarked, 'To succeed with the opposite sex, tell her you're impotent. She can't wait to disprove it'?

(a) Percy Aldridge Grainger (b) Cary Grant (c) Woody Allen (d) Groucho Marx

584. Who wrote, 'Is it not strange that desire should so many years outlive performance'?

(a) Dante (b) James Joyce (c) Percy Bysshe Shelley (d) Shakespeare

585. Who said regarding certain coital positions, 'Certainly nothing is unnatural that is not physically impossible'?

(a) Richard Brinsley Sheridan (b) Ugo Betti (c) Mae West (d) Marilyn Monroe

586. Who said, 'If a woman hasn't got a tiny streak of a harlot in her, she's a dry stick as a rule'?

(a) Michel de Montaigne (b) Nietzsche (c) D.H. Lawrence (d) H.L. Mencken

587. Who said, 'Sex is the great amateur art. The professional, male or female, is frowned on; he or she misses the whole point and spoils the show'?

(a) David Cort (b) Billy Boy Franklin (c) Jawaharlal Nehru (d) Clarence Darrow

588. Who said, 'The sexual embrace can only be compared with music and with prayer'?

(a) Mahatma Gandhi (b) Havelock Ellis (c) Lord Birkett (d) La Rochefoucauld

589. Who said, 'You know women as well as I do. They are only willing when you compel them, but after that they're as enthusiastic as you are'?

(a) Jean Giraudoux (b) Truman Capote (c) Karl Kraus (d) Omar Sharif

590. Which great philosopher said, 'There is no greater or keener pleasure than that of bodily love — and none which is more irrational'?

(a) Socrates (b) Bertrand Russell (c) Plato (d) Nietzsche

591. Who said, 'Marriage is the only adventure open to the timid'?

(a) Voltaire (b) Beaumarchais (c) Mark Twain (d) Machiavelli

592. Who said, 'There may be good, but there are no pleasant marriages'?

(a) John Stuart Mill (b) Charles Lamb (c) Francis Bacon (d) La Rochefoucauld

593. Who said, 'More things belong to marriage than four bare legs in a bed'?

(a) John Heywood (b) Seneca (c) Logan Pearsall Smith (d) Samuel Johnson

594. Who said, 'Hanging and marriage go by destiny'?

(a) Schopenhauer (b) Mark Twain (c) George Farquhar (d) Cervantes

595. Who said disparagingly of marriage, 'A system could not well have been devised more studiously hostile to human happiness than marriage'?

(a) Shakespeare (b) Thomas Haliburton (c) Voltaire (d) Shelley

596. Who said, 'Love is an egoism of two'?

(a) William Hazlitt (b) Antoigne de la Sale (c) La Rochefoucauld (d) Hugo Grotius

597. Who remarked, 'Love is nothing save an insatiate thirst to enjoy a greedily desired object'?

(a) Montaigne (b) Artemus Ward (c) Mahatma Gandhi (d) Acharya Vinoba Bhave

598. Who said, 'To be in love is merely to be in a state of perpetual anaesthesis — to mistake an ordinary young man for a Greek god or an ordinary young woman for a goddess.'?

(a) Santayana (b) Thorstein Vebler (c) H.L. Mencken (d) Voltaire

599. Who made this funny remark, "Marriage is the net in which the jade snares the jaded"?

(a) P.G. Wodehouse (b) Oscar Wilde (c) Ogden Nash (d) J.K. Galbraith

600. Who remarked, 'It is a woman's business to get married as soon as possible; and a man's to keep unmarried as long as he can'?

(a) Niels Bohr (b) Dev Anand (c) Sheila Graham (d) George Bernard Shaw

601. Who said, 'Marriage is a bribe to make a housekeeper think she's a householder'?

(a) G.J. Nathan (b) Bertrand Russell (c) Thornton Wilder (d) Havelock Ellis

602. Who said, 'Love is like a coconut which is good while it is fresh, but you have to spit it out when the juice is gone, what's left tastes bitter'?

(a) Bertolt Brecht (b) Samuel Beckett (c) D.H. Lawrence (d) Dorothy Parker

603. Who said in 1976, 'I'll wager you that in ten years it will be fashionable again to be a virgin'?

(a) Allen Ginsberg (b) Christopher Fry (c) Anthony Burgess (d) Barbara Cartland

604. Who made this interesting comment regarding sex, 'The pleasure is momentary, the position ridiculous and the expense damnable'?

(a) Alan Valentine (b) Henry E. Sigerist (c) Earl of Chesterfield (d) François Rabelais

605. Who said, 'Sexuality is the lyricism of the masses'?

(a) Victor Hugo (b) Charles Baudelaire (c) Sir Thomas Browne (d) Anna Chamber

606. Who remarked, 'No sex is better than bad sex'?

(a) Germaine Greer (b) Ben Hecht (c) Celsus (d) Prem Chopra

607. Who remarked, 'Sometimes I wish I could fall in love. Then at least you know who your opponent is'?

(a) Woody Allen (b) Christopher Morley (c) Lewis Carroll (d) Peter Ustinov

608. Who made this interesting remark, 'I can understand companionship. I can understand bought sex in the afternoon. I cannot understand the love affair'?

(a) Karl Popper (b) Beaumarchais (c) Henry Miller (d) Gore Vidal

609. Who remarked, 'Marriage is a great institution, but I'm not ready for an institution yet'?

(a) Mata Hari (b) Indira Gandhi, before her marriage to Feroze Gandhi (c) Mae West (d) Pooja Bedi

610. Who said regarding marriage, 'There are four stages to a marriage. First there's the affair, then the marriage, then children and finally the fourth stage, without which you cannot know a woman, the divorce'?

(a) Norman Mailer (b) Blaise Pascal (c) G.K. Chesterton (d) Goldie Hawn

611. He came to believe in a strong bisexual aspect in every personality, and said, 'Every sexual act is one between four individuals.' Who was he?

(a) Carl Jung (b) Sigmund Freud (c) Alfred Adler (d) Christian Barnard

612. This famous courtesan was a compulsive gambler and lost an estimated $ 20 million at the casino. When asked what she would have otherwise done with that money, she replied, 'I might have endowed a university for prostitutes. Think of the variety of courses we could have offered.' Who was she?

(a) La Belle Otero (b) Cora Pearl (c) Valeria Messalina (d) Christine Keeler

613. When someone taunted him that he would probably die by the hangman's noose or a vile disease, he retorted with this famous remark, "Sir, that depends upon whether I embrace your principles or your mistress." Who was this witty person?

(a) William Gladstone (b) Benjamin Disraeli (c) William Douglas (d) Mark Twain

614. Which famous person, one month after his marriage, told his young wife, "Mamie, there's one thing you must understand. My country comes first and always will. You come second." Who was this patriot?

(a) Dwight David Eisenhower (b) George Washington (c) John Fitzgerald Kennedy (d) Theodore Roosevelt

615. His wealthy pupil Jane Stirling tried to marry him but he remarked, 'I would as soon marry death.' Who was he?

(a) Voltaire (b) Leonardo da Vinci (c) Frédéric François Chopin (d) Peter Paul Rubens

616. When he was told that Alfonso d'Este, his son-in-law, besides making love to his daughter nightly, was making love with equal regularity to other women during the day, he replied, 'well, he is young, and that is how it should be.' Who was this wise father?

(a) Alexander VI (b) Alfred the Great (c) Robert Belinsky (d) Alphonse Daudet

617. Her rival actress had been presented by her lover with a magnificient diamond necklace, which being too long was disappearing down her cleavage. Sarcastically she remarked, 'well, it's just returning to its source'. Who is she?

(a) Mae West (b) Marilyn Monroe (c) Sophie Arnould (d) Jane Russell

618. Which British Prime Minister, during a visit to America, sent a magnificient orchid to his hostess along with a card saying, 'I would be most obliged if you would pin this on your white meat'?

(a) David Lloyd-George (b) Harold Macmillan (c) Benjamin Disraeli (d) Winston Churchill

619. Before the first night of his play a pretty young actress, besieged with stage fright, rushed to him and asked him to feel her heart. When she pursued, 'How does it feel?' he replied, 'Round'. Who is this playwright?

(a) Alexandre Dumas (fils) (b) Shakespeare (c) Samuel Beckett (d) Molière

620. Her sexual expertise was so renowned that daughters of the aristocracy were sent to her to learn the art of love. When one of her students asked, 'How large should a woman's breast be to attract a lover?', she replied, 'Large enough to fill the hand of a man.' Who was this famous courtesan?

(a) Kitty Fisher (b) La Belle Otero (c) Harriette Wilson (d) Ninon de Lenclos

621. At a banquet this Pope was sitting next to a young lady wearing an extremely low-cut dress. After some time he offered the lady an apple and when she refused, he urged, 'Please do take it, madam. It was only after Eve ate the apple that she became aware of how little she had on.' Who was this Pope of the Roman Church?

(a) Clement XI (b) Innocent XI (c) Pius X (d) John XXIII

622. When Nancy Astor became the first woman to take a seat in the British House of Commons in 1919, this male parliamentarian, who later became Prime Minister could not stand it. He remarked, 'I find your intrusion into the all-male preserve embarrassing — as embarrassing as if you have burst into my bathroom when I have nothing on.' Who was this parliamentarian?

(a) Winston Churchill (b) Stanley Baldwin (c) James Ramsay MacDonald (d) Neville Chamberlain

623. When she was asked her opinion about Philip Roth, who had just completed a book on masturbation, she replied, 'He's a fine writer, but I wouldn't want to shake hands with him.' Who was she?

(a) Helen Tamiris (b) Laurette Taylor (c) Dame Ellen Terry (d) Jacqueline Susann

624. Who made this famous remark, 'He that falls in love with himself will have no rivals'?

(a) Benjamin Franklin (b) Oscar Wilde (c) Phyllis Diller (d) Mark Twain

625. Which famous actress said, "Sex is an emotion in motion"?

(a) Tallulah Bankhead (b) Mae West (c) Marilyn Monroe (d) Greta Garbo

626. This short story writer and doyen of minor light verse and wit went on her honeymoon. When her editor Harold Ross began pressuring her for her belated copy, she replied with this famous remark, 'Too fucking busy, and vice versa.' Who was this witty lady?

(a) Dorothy Parker (b) Katherine Mansfield (c) Pearl Buck (d) Jacqueline Susann

627. Who said, 'A girl must marry for love, and keep on marrying until she finds it'?

(a) Elizabeth Taylor (b) Marilyn Monroe (c) Mae West (d) Zsa Zsa Gabor

628. Who said, 'When women kiss, it always reminds me of prize-fighters shaking hands'?

(a) Heinrich Heine (b) H.L. Mencken (c) Oscar Wilde (d) Groucho Marx

629. About whom did Dorothy Parker say, 'He and I had an office so tiny that an inch smaller and it would have been adultery'?

(a) Cleveland Amory (b) Ernest Hemingway (c) Robert Benchley (d) Harold Ross

630. Actor Donald Sutherland was once making up in his dressing room when he heard a noise behind him. Turning around, he was astonished to see a famous

actress stark naked. Seeing him surprised, she asked, 'What's the matter darling? Haven't you ever seen a blonde before?' Who was this actress?

(a) Tallulah Bankhead (b) Mae West (c) Marlene Dietrich (d) Clara Bow

631. About this famous empress, a contemporary once said, '. . . far-sighted nature had placed the wherewithal to pay her bills beneath her navel. . .' Who was this famous empress?

(a) Catherine the Great (b) Agrippina (c) Marie Antoinette (d) Joséphine de Beauharnais

632. Who commented upon Napoleon's sexual prowess thus, 'Bon-a-parte est Bon-à-rien', meaning 'Bonaparte is good-for-nothing'?

(a) His wife Joséphine (b) His personal orderly Gaspard Gourgard (c) His chief aide-de-camp Duroc (d) His mistress Marie Antoinette Duchatel

633. When her jilted lover Robert Savage, a millionaire's son, tried to kill himself by slashing his wrists, she exclaimed, 'Jesus Christ, he's got to be kidding. Men don't slash their wrists, they use a gun'. Who was she?

(a) Marlene Dietrich (b) Mata Hari (c) Mae West (d) Clara Bow

634. In the film *Caligula,* a Penthouse Pet had to piss on an actor two times, but she did it three times. Seeing this, the director screamed at her, 'For Chrissakes, you want to be an actress but you can't even take a "don't piss" direction!' Who was he?

(a) Tinto Brass (b) Victor Fleming (c) John Gilbert (d) Gilbert Roland

635. When an art critic called him 'sexless and unclean' he replied, 'As to my uncleanliness I do the best for it in my morning bath, and if he has really any doubts as to my sex, he may come and see me take it.' Who was he?

(a) Auguste Renoir (b) Vincent Van Gogh (c) Pablo Picasso (d) Aubrey Beardsley

636. Who said, 'The way in which people make love may tell us more about them than any searching analysis could'?

(a) Maurice Nadeau (b) Sigmund Freud (c) Karen Horney (d) Alfred Adler

637. Who said, 'The idea of using censors to bar thoughts of sex is dangerous. A person without sex thoughts is abnormal'?

(a) Johann Wolfgang von Goethe (b) Ernest Hemingway (c) J. Edgar Hoover (d) William O. Douglas

638. Which U.S. President said, 'Blondes have the hottest kisses. Redheads are fair-to-middling torrid, and brunettes are the frigidest of all'?

(a) Ronald Reagan (b) William Howard Taft (c) Andrew Johnson (d) Richard Nixon

639. Who commented on the growing trend to theatrical nudity, 'Soon the actors will be all nude, the audience will be all nude, everyone will be nude except the police'?

(a) Rex Harrison (b) Margaret Mitchell (c) Jacqueline Susann (d) Gypsy Rose Lee

640. Who said, 'If you use sex for fun, it is virtue; if you use it for reproduction, it is sin'?

(a) Mae West (b) Robert Ludlum (c) Acharya Rajneesh (d) Elizabeth Taylor

641. Who said on pornography, 'I never understood why censors were so interested in trying to suppress anything which has to do with sex and nothing which has to do with violence, with dishonesty in any form'?

(a) Mark Twain (b) George Bernard Shaw (c) Mae West (d) Maurice Girodias

642. Who said about a rival actress, 'She reminds me of those nations that are always extending their boundaries but can not retain their conquests'?

(a) Sophie Arnould (b) Mae West (c) Racquel Welch (d) Sharmila Tagore

643. Who said in his old age, 'As a young man I used to have four supple members and one stiff one. Now I have four stiff and one supple'?

(a) Mark Twain (b) Oscar Wilde (c) George Bernard Shaw (d) Henri Duc d'Aumale

644. Her roles had such display of passion, that once even her admirer complained that she could not bring her daughter to her plays. To this, the famous actress remarked, 'But, madame, you should remember that were it not for passion, you would have no daughter to bring.' Who was she?

(a) Sarah Bernhardt (b) Bo Derek (c) Anne Sheridan (d) Helen

645. Who said, 'All I can say is that sex in Ireland is as yet in its infancy'?

(a) Charles Parnell (b) William Gladstone (c) Jack Lynch (d) Eamon de Valera

646. Who said, 'The trouble with the censor is that he worries if a girl has a cleavage. He should worry if she hasn't any'?

(a) Protima Bedi (b) Jay Shree T. (c) Marilyn Monroe (d) Raj Kapoor

647. Who said, 'The civilization is decaying, going down the bottomless pit, down the chasm. And believe me, the only bridge across the chasm will be the phallus'?

(a) Casanova (b) Aubrey Beardsley (c) Mark Twain (d) D.H. Lawrence

648. She had many lovers during her life and observed, 'It is by spending oneself that one becomes rich'. Who was she?

(a) Sarah Bernhardt (b) Mata Hari (c) Mae West (d) Cleopatra

649. Who said, 'The surest way to the soul is through the flesh'?

(a) T.E. Lawrence (b) Bobby Fischer (c) Mark Twain (d) Mabel Dodge Luhan

650. Who exclaimed, 'My breasts are like towers; then was I in his sight as one that found favour; a bundle of myrrh is my well-beloved one unto me; he shall lie all night betwixt my breasts.'?

(a) Mae West (b) The bride in Song of Solomon (c) Twelve-year-old Dolores Haze in *Lolita* (d) Paul Morel's mother in *Sons and Lovers*

651. This famous lady posed as goddess Venus for the Italian sculptor Canova. When the work was exhibited, one of her shocked friends asked how she could pose like that and calm came the reply, 'The studio was kept very comfortably warm.' Identify the lady.

(a) Pauline Bonaparte Borghese (b) Mona Lisa del Gioconda (c) Constanza d'Avalos (d) Anne Boleyn

652. Who said in *Proverbs* 'Rejoice with the wife of thy youth; let her breasts satisfy thee at all times; and be thou ravished always with her love.'?

(a) David (b) Goliath (c) Solomon (d) Queen of Sheba

653. He loved the famous Greek courtesan Lais. When someone told him that she didn't love him, he replied calmly, 'That doesn't matter to me. I don't suppose fish or wines love me either. But I take pleasure in both all the same.' Who was this philosopher?

(a) Socrates (b) Xenophon (c) Plutarch (d) Aristippus of Cyrene

654. This famous Athenian general was the son of the illustrious commander Conon and a courtesan. When someone chided him for being the son of a courtesan he replied with this famous retort, 'I'm very grateful to my mother for having made me the son of Conon'. Who was he?

(a) Pericles (b) Alexander the Great (c) Xenophon (d) Timotheus

655. This English Prime Minister, towards the end of his life was once sitting in the House of Commons smoking room with his fly-buttons undone. When this was pointed out to him, he said, 'Dead birds don't fall out of nests.' Who was he?

(a) William Gladstone (b) Winston Churchill (c) Harold Macmillan (d) Stanley Baldwin

656. Which Latin poet when derided for his bawdy poetry, exclaimed, 'But my poems, just like an amorous husband, must have some spermatozoa.'?

(a) Martial (b) Ovid (c) Pliny, the Younger (d) Lucretius

657. Who said about nudism, 'It is a reaction against the abuse of clothes which has produced unnatural excess of sexual desire'?

(a) Albert Camus (b) Dwight D. Eisenhower (c) George Bernard Shaw (d) Lily Langtry

658. Which famous film star said, 'Sex appeal is fifty percent what you've got and fifty percent what people think you've got'?

(a) Clara Bow (b) Jayshree T. (c) Sri Devi (d) Sophia Loren

659. Which film star said, 'It's an extra dividend when you like the girl you're in love with'?

(a) Groucho Marx (b) Clark Gable (c) Johny Walker (d) Shashi Kapoor

660. Which film star said, 'A man in love is incomplete until he is married. Then he is finished'?

(a) Zsa Zsa Gabor (b) Katharine Hepburn (c) Elizabeth Taylor (d) Kishore Kumar

661. Who said, 'The difference between sex and death is that with death you can do it alone and no one is going to make fun of you'?

(a) Joseph Heller (b) Will Hay (c) Groucho Marx (d) Woody Allen

662. Who said, 'As for that topsy-turvy tangle known as *soixante-neuf,* personally I have always felt it to be madly confusing, like trying to pat your head and rub your stomach at the same time'?

(a) Roger Daltrey (b) W.H. Auden (c) Helen Lawrenson (d) Erica Jong

663. Who said, 'A woman occasionally is quite a serviceable substitute for masturbation. It takes an abundance of imagination, to be sure'?

(a) W.H. Auden (b) Karl Kraus (c) Bob Hope (d) Groucho Marx

664. Who said, 'I'll bet £5 that any man visiting a naturist club for the first time *couldn't* get an erection'?

(a) Charlie Chaplin (b) Woodrow Wilson (c) Jack Wrate (d) Aneurin Bevan

665. She was known to have many lovers, yet all her five children bore remarkable similarity to her husband. When someone expressed his surprise at it, she remarked, 'I am careful never to take a passenger except when the vessel is full.' Who was she?

(a) Julia (b) Agrippina (c) Catherine the Great (d) Sarah Bernhardt

666. Who said, 'Sex is like money — very nice to have but vulgar to talk about'?

(a) Saul Bellow (b) Anita Bryant (c) Truman Capote (d) Tonia Berg

21
SEXUALLY TRANSMITTED DISEASES

667. What is the name given to the speciality of medicine, which aims to study and treat the sexually transmitted diseases?

(a) Sexology (b) Venereology (c) Dermatology (d) No name is given to this speciality

668. Which venereal disease is commonly known as 'the clap'?

(a) Gonorrhoea (b) Syphilis (c) Lymphogranuloma venerum (d) Non-specific urethritis

669. Gonorrhoea is caused by a

(a) Virus (b) Fungus (c) Bacteria (d) Protozoa

670. The word gonorrhoea comes from two Greek words meaning

(a) the flow of pus (b) the flow of seed (c) a debauched person (d) a sexual adventurer

671. We are all aware of the disease small pox. But which disease was referred to as the great pox, or simply, pox?

(a) Syphilis (b) Gonorrhoea (c) Chancroid (d) Lymphogranuloma venerum

672. Which horrifying venereal disease first appeared in Portugal in 1494?

(a) Gonorrhoea (b) Chancroid (c) Genital herpes (d) Syphilis

673. Which venereal disease is caused by a virus?

(a) Syphilis (b) Chancroid (c) Lymphogranuloma venerum (d) Nonspecific urethritis

674. Gonorrhoea usually causes inflammation of the urethra. If the inflammation is caused by something other than gonorrhoea it is known as

(a) Syphilis (b) NGU (c) non-specific pruritis (d) LGV

675. Which ancient civilization, towards the end of its influence, referred to all diseases of the sexual parts as *morbus indecens* or indecent diseases?

(a) Romans (b) Greeks (c) Etruscans (d) Hittites

676. Which sexually transmitted disease is caused by *Donovania granulomatis*?

(a) Herpes Zoster (b) Lymphogranuloma venerum (c) Granuloma inguinale (d) Chancroid

677. Which sexually transmitted disease is caused by Ducrey's bacillus?

(a) Donovanosis (b) Cryptosporidiosis (c) Chancroid (d) Listeriosis

678. AIDS is a dreadful disease mainly transmitted by sexual intercourse. Under which other circumstances can AIDS spread or be transmitted?

(a) Sharing needles for drug injection (b) Transfusion of infected blood (c) Bites by infected mosquitoes (d) Transmission from infected mother to the newborn

679. Who is generally credited with the discovery and isolation of AIDS virus?

(a) Professor Luc Montaignier (b) Robert Gallo (c) Jean-Lous Brunet (d) Massachusetts Institute of Technology (MIT)

680. Which famous Hollywood actor died of AIDS?

(a) Gary Cooper (b) Errol Flynn (c) Omar Sharif (d) Rock Hudson

681. When did the United Nations observe the World AIDS Day?

(a) January 30, 1991 (b) March 3, 1991 (c) December 1,1991 (d) December 31, 1991

682. According to official data on AIDS, how many people in India were confirmed to have been infected with HIV virus till October 31, 1991?

(a) 131 (b) 1031 (c) 3179 (d) 6106

683. In which year was AIDS first detected?

(a) 1970 (b) 1977 (c) 1981 (d) 1986

684. Who said regarding AIDS, 'If you were the devil, you couldn't conceive of a disease that would be more disruptive and disturbing than this one. It could prove to be the plague of the millennium'?

(a) Ronald Reagan (b) Robert Gallo (c) Rock Hudson (d) Dr. Alvin Friedman-kien

22
HAZY AREAS

685. We are familiar with *hijras* who amuse the crowd with their dance and lewd gestures on occasions of gaiety. Biologically what are they?

(a) Males who have been deprived of their external genitalia before the age of puberty (b) Females whose clitoris and vulva have been surgically excised (c) Individuals born with one testis and one ovary (d) Individuals whose testes and ovaries do not function.

686. And who are the *Zananas*?

(a) Female prostitutes living as males (b) Males who dress as females and acquire mannerisms of females (c) Males who have lost their external genitalia much after puberty as in an accident (d) Individuals having four ovaries, thus showing signs of a 'superfemale'

687. In this genetic disorder, the male has underdeveloped testes and his seminal fluid contains no spermatozoon. It is caused by an extra X-chromosome, which he accidentally inherits from his parents. Name this condition.

(a) Down's syndrome (b) Kleine-Levin syndrome (c) Cri-du-chat syndrome (d) Klinefelter's syndrome

688. In this genetic disorder, the female does not menstruate at all. She remains a dwarf and does not develop external bodily features of a woman. It is due to the absence of a second X-chromosome which all females normally have. Name this disorder.

(a) Down's syndrome (b) Katayama syndrome (c) Turner's syndrome (d) Pineal syndrome

689. What is the technical term for sex-change operation?

(a) Sex eversion (b) Sex inversion (c) Sexual orthoptic surgery (d) Sex transplantation

690. Why is the name of George Jamieson immortal in the history of sex?

(a) Doctors could not determine his true sex (b) His was the most celebrated case of sex-change surgery (c) He had the largest male organ (21", at rest) according to the *Guinness Book of World Records* (d) He was the only person to have two peckers

691. Which Danish surgeon was among the first to successfully accomplish sex change surgery and was so inundated with requests subsequently that Danish law had to be changed to exclude non-Danish patients?

(a) Fredrik Bajer (b) Johannes Vilhelm Jensen (c) Henrik Pontoppidan (d) Christian Hamburger

23

SLANG AND EUPHEMISM

692. Touching the tip of the thumb to the end of one's nose and spreading the fingers wide is a rude gesture known as

(a) Anne's fan (b) finger fan (c) fannerism (d) symbolic sex

693. A sadistic male who derives special pleasure from beating up homosexual males is known as

(a) skinny dip (b) sissy-beater (c) teapot lid (d) buster

694. A skin magazine is a magazine which

(a) shows how to keep your skin healthy (b) shows the various anatomical features of skin (c) is made from the skin of animals (d) features male and female nudes

695. A buffarilla is a

(a) sexy young man (b) sexy young woman (c) ugly young woman (d) ugly young man

696. In slang what does downshire mean?

(a) Male organ (b) Hips (c) Female pubic hair (d) Oversized breasts

697. What is a dreadnought?

(a) A naked female (b) Condom (c) A handkerchief soaked with human semen (d) A contraceptive pill

698. What or who is a fishwife?

(a) A woman shared between five or more males (b) A woman who prefers oral sex (c) A woman who is frigid (d) The female wife or consort of a homosexual male

699. If a female is flashing her bubs, what is she doing?

(a) Giving signal that she is ready for sex (b) Exposing her breasts (c) Rebutting your sexual advances (d) Asking you to perform anal sex

700. What or who is a flaming queen?

(a) A menstruating woman (b) A woman with very gaudy make up (c) A very obvious and exaggeratedly effeminate male homosexual (d) A woman who is sexually aroused

701. If a female has a bun in the oven, what description suits her best?

(a) She is pregnant (b) She is a bad cook (c) She prefers oral sex (d) She has only one breast

702. What are the gazongas?

(a) Undersized breasts (b) Very sexy cheeks (c) Extremely well-shaped breasts (d) Extremely sexy lips

703. What is a pansyland?

(a) Brothel (b) A place where an unmarried boy and a girl have intercourse (c) Normally a jail where female prisoners engage in lesbian activities (d) A gathering place for homosexual males

704. What are the parentheses?

(a) Female genitals (b) Female breasts (c) Female buttocks (d) Female pubic hair

705. If someone cracks a Judy's teacup, what does he do?

(a) Performs oral sex (b) Deflowers a virgin (c) Beats a woman to get sexual pleasure (d) Asks a woman to take alcohol to arouse her

706. What are the whirligigs?

(a) Female breasts (b) Hymen (c) Human testes (d) Male hips

707. If somebody is tipping the velvet, what is he doing?

(a) Caressing his wife's breasts (b) Kissing a girl passionately on the breasts (c) Kissing a girl with the tongue entering her mouth (d) Stroking a girl's hips

708. Who in slang is a fresh cow?

(a) A newly married woman (b) A recently delivered mother (c) A virgin (d) A man with a fresh attack of gonorrhoea

709. What do you get or hire from a molly-house?

(a) Prostitutes (b) Young boys for homosexual activity (c) Electrical gadgets to satisfy sexual urges (d) Erotic songs recorded on tapes

710. What does 'flashing' mean?

(a) Showing one's teeth to a buxom girl (b) Wiggling an ear at an old woman (c) Switching a light on and off in order to give one's girl friend a secret message (d) Showing one's genitals to a member of the opposite sex

711. Which of the following is a slang term for bisexuality?

(a) AC-DC (b) Gerry (c) Peckerwood (d) Geld

712. Which part of the female anatomy is often known as 'the old man in the boat'?

(a) Nipples (b) Anus (c) Clitoris (d) Navel

713. The word dildo, meaning artificial penis, comes from

(a) an Italian word meaning 'delight' (b) A Malay word meaning 'rod' (c) A Hawaiian word meaning 'heaven' (d) An esperanto word meaning 'ocean of joy'

714. This word for a mistress comes from *Merry Wives of Windsor* by Shakespeare. Identify it.

(a) Concubine (b) Strumpet (c) Gallimaufrey (d) Gardenia

715. This word for a prostitute comes from *All's Well That Ends Well* by Shakespeare. Identify it.

(a) Whore (b) Gamester (c) Faggot (d) Tottie

716. A homosexual male who derives special satisfaction from masturbating others is called

(a) a mitten queen (b) a mollycoddle (c) Mister Tom (d) Mister Alcrity

717. What is an urning?

(a) An urn showing nude females (b) A vase in the shape of a nude female (c) Euphemism for homosexual; very popular in Victorian times (d) A slang term for prostitutes during Edwardian times

718. 'To goose' means

(a) thrusting of a finger at the cleavage of a person's buttocks (b) grasping of another person's genitalia from behind (c) pumping breasts of a female (d) slapping the buttocks of a homosexual partner

719. What was the name given to the fictitious central part of a ship, which was used by homosexual sailors to lure new recruits down into the hold of the ship, where they could then be assaulted without fear of interruption?

(a) Silver mast (b) Gay sails (c) Gay plimsoll (d) Golden rivet

720. A man who lives off a woman or women by performing sexual and/or social favours for her, such as dancing with her for a fee, is known as a

(a) gigolo (b) pimp (c) shrimp (d) boot

721. What is Roman charity?

(a) Kissing naked buttocks of a female (b) Breast-feeding an adult (c) Group sex (d) Sex with animals

24
MOVIES

722. In which famous love-movie did Leela Chitnis and Ashok Kumar act together?

(a) *Dil Tera Deewana* (b) *Neecha Nagar* (c) *Achhut Kanya* (d) *Prem Nagar*

723. The film *Manoranjan* depicted Zeenat Aman as a prostitute. On which famous English movie was it based?

(a) *Irma La Douce* (b) *Dial M for Murder* (c) *A Prostitute's Story* (d) *Red light Area*

724. Her films include the Oscar-winning *Two Women* (1960), and *Marriage Italian Style* (1964). Her role with Peter Sellers in *The Millionairess* (1960), proved that she was a skilled comedienne. Who was this sex symbol and superstar?

(a) Tallulah Bankhead (b) Ursula Anderss (c) Bo Derek (d) Sophia Loren

725. She played a brilliant role in Louis Malle's *Pretty Baby* as a teeny bopper prostitute. That was when she was 12 only, and her climb to fame had begun. Who was this sex symbol?

(a) Farah Diba (b) Brooke Shields (c) Sophia Loren (d) Ursula Anderss

726. Which erotic movie star became renowned for her performance in *Deep Throat*?

(a) Bo Derek (b) Anne Sheridan (c) Linda Lovelace (d) Sophia Loren

727. Which was the most successful pornographic film to be shown in America?

(a) *Sex, Sex, Sex* (b) *No Sex Please, We Are Americans* (c) *Sex from Bed to Grave* (d) *Deep Throat*

728. Who acted as Rakhi's lover in Aparna Sen's film *Paroma*?

(a) Ajit Vacchani (b) Mukul Sharma (c) Pankaj Kapur (d) Dilip Dhawan

729. Which movie features the longest kiss in motion picture history?

(a) *You're in the Army Now* (b) *Gone With the Wind* (c) *Ben Hur* (d) *Love Story*

730. More than 300 women auditioned for parts in this film by performing in sexual screen tests so that the director could see 'Not just whether, but how are

they good at it? Do they fuck cheerfully or not?' Which was the film?

(a) *Blow Hot Blow Cold* (b) *Deep Throat* (c) *The Sexual Extravaganza* (d) *Caligula*

731. Her first movie *The Outlaw* was delayed for three years as a result of censorship hurdles. Who is she?

(a) Anne Sheridan (b) Marlene Dietrich (c) Jane Russell (d) Clara Bow

732. In which of Bergman's films, is the highly controversial scene of a sister making love to her young brother in the waterlogged interior of a grounded boat shown?

(a) *Through a Glass Darkly* (b) *The Virgin Spring* (c) *The Seventh Seal* (d) *Cries and Whispers*

25
LEGENDARY CREATURES

733. These beautiful women were human from the waist up, but fish from the waist down and were usually seen sitting on rocks near the sea shore combing their long golden hair. Who are these legendary creatures?

(a) Medusa (b) Mermaids (c) Sphinx (d) Sirens

734. The comb of the creatures mentioned above was made up of

(a) sand (b) sea shells (c) fishbone (d) whalebone

735. Sometimes a man could turn a mermaid into an ordinary woman and make her his wife. How could he do it?

(a) By seizing her comb (b) By cutting her from waist downwards (c) By a special incantation (d) By making her pregnant

736. Mermaids could sometimes apparently take on full human form by themselves, come ashore for a time and might even go into a village to join in a dance. How could a clever villager say that she was not a real woman, but a mermaid?

(a) By looking at her fish-like eyes (b) By noticing scales on her toes (c) By smelling salt on her body

(d) By seeing that the bottom of her dress was dripping sea water

737. A statue of a mermaid sits at the harbour entrance of a country symbolizing the port's seafaring tradition. Which country?

(a) Germany (b) Netherlands (c) Denmark (d) Egypt

738. Which sculptor made *The Little Mermaid* mentioned above?

(a) Joseph Utzon (b) Edvard Eriksen (c) Prashanta Kumar Bhattacharya (d) Barbara Hepworth

739. Which mythological goat-legged lechers, who are ever-aroused and ever-potent have given rise to a medical term describing insatiable, lust-ridden, and sexually aggressive men?

(a) Titans (b) Circe (c) Sirens (d) Satyrs

26

THE LAWS

740. Among which ancient community, if a woman touched the genitals of her husband, the offending hand had to be amputated according to the existing laws?

(a) Hittites (b) Jews (c) Mayas (d) Aztecs

741. According to Indian law if someone outrages the modesty of a woman by using criminal force, what is the maximum period for which he may be imprisoned?

(a) 14 days (b) 1 year (c) 2 years (d) 5 years

742. In which section of the Indian Penal Code, has the punishment for outraging the modesty of a woman been prescribed?

(a) 354 (b) 375 (c) 376 (d) 420

743. What is the maximum punishment prescribed for a person who outrages the modesty of a woman by uttering lewd words, making vulgar gestures or exhibiting obscene objects?

(a) 14 days (b) 1 year (c) 2 years (d) 5 years

744. In which section of the Indian Penal Code is the above punishment prescribed?

(a) 375 (b) 376 (c) 420 (d) 509

27
GREAT SENSUALISTS

745. Which eighteenth century adventurer and seducer has recorded his exploits in a twelve-volume work called *Memoirs*?

(a) Don Juan (b) Giacomo Girolamo Casanova (c) Grigori Rasputin (d) Earl of Rochester

746. Who was the earliest known erotic artist?

(a) Elephantis (b) Cleopatra (c) Zandra (d) Aretino

747. Henry VIII, the king of England, was a very sensual man and had many wives. Which of the following were Henry VIII's wives?

(a) Catherine of Aragon (b) Anne Boleyn (c) Jane Seymour (d) Anne of Cleves

748. King Charles II said of him that 'Nature had given him a patent to be Apollo's viceroy.' Who was he?

(a) Edward Sellon (b) Sir Charles Sedley (c) Casanova (d) Don Juan

749. She was the third wife of Emperor Claudius of Rome and was notorious for her cruelty and insatiable sexual appetite. Who was she?

(a) Valerina (b) Catherina (c) Jacobine (d) Messalina

750. He awarded his crew a badge of honour — a metal image of an erect penis and testicles — to sport on their lapels and kept a record of their nightly conquests. Who was he?

(a) King Nebuchadnezzar (b) Errol Flynn (c) John Barrymore (d) Aristotle Ulysses Onassis

751. Which famous actress is reputed to have made love to the entire football team of the University of Southern California, on a regular basis at her Beverly Hills home?

(a) Clara Bow (b) Zsa Zsa Gabor (c) Marilyn Monroe (d) Marlene Dietrich

752. Who is said to have seduced the Empress Anne of Russia while disguised as King Charles XII of Sweden?

(a) Casanova (b) Don Juan (c) Sir Francis Dashwood (d) Sir Francis Drake

753. This British actress and famous beauty was the daughter of the Dean of Jersey of whom she later said, "He was a damned nuisance. He couldn't be trusted with any woman anywhere." Who is she?

(a) Billie Holliday (b) Lily Langtry (c) Natalie Barney (d) Cora Pearl

754. This British M.P. was a collector of pornography. His country seat at Fryston Hall, Yorkshire, was known as Aphrodisiopolis because of its fine, vast collection of erotic books and illustrations. Who was he?

(a) Viscount Melbourne (b) William Pitt (c) George Grenville (d) Richard Monckton Milnes

755. Aristocratic young men of the seventeenth and eighteenth centuries who prided themselves on their amorous adventures were called

(a) rakes (b) male whores (c) yuppies (d) dongs

756. She was born in Florence, married a French king, and was blamed for encouraging perversion at court. Who was she?

(a) Anne Boleyn (b) Catherine, the Great (c) Catherine de Medici (d) Alexandra II

757. He was the Victorian publisher of pornography who operated in London in the nineteenth century. During his forty years in the pornographic trade he suffered nine convictions. Who was he?

(a) Sir Francis Dashwood (b) William Dugdale (c) Norman Prince (d) William Chatto

758. He was Nero's adviser in all matters including the sexual. Nero, with a jaded appetite for sex would regard nothing as enjoyable unless he had given his sanction to it. Who was he?

(a) Cicero (b) Plutonius (c) Aretonius (d) Petronius Arbiter

759. This Victorian collector of erotica and pornography asked his friend Sir Richard Burton to bring him

back a girl's skin from Africa, taken from a living victim. Who was he?

(a) Frederick Hankey (b) Sir Francis Monckton (c) Peter Marsh (d) Lord Dennison

760. This British writer, adventurer, and womanizer, caught the housemaid in bed with a man at the age of four, examined girls' legs at five and felt his sisters' breasts at eleven. He recounted his unique experiences in the book *My Life and Loves* (1923-27). Who are we talking about?

(a) Rex Harrison (b) Sir Charles Sedley (c) Frank Harris (d) The Earl of Rochester

761. Which famous writer spent all his spare time photographing little girls, often in the nude, but lost interest in them when they began to show signs of puberty?

(a) Lewis Carroll (b) Vladimir Nabokov (c) William Somerset Maugham (d) James Joyce

762. Which famous English pornographer has written the erotic autobiography *The Ups and Downs of Life (1867)*?

(a) Sir Charles Sedley (b) Edward Sellon (c) Walter (d) George Whitmore

763. This nineteenth century Victorian collector of erotica also collected less prurient books including works on Cervantes. He bequeathed his entire collection of 15,229 books to the British Museum — making the Cervantes bequest conditional on acceptance of the erotica. Name him.

(a) April Ashley (b) Marvin Ziporyn (c) Norman Wight (d) Henry Spencer Ashbee

764. This religious crank set up the Agapemone or "Abode of Love" in Somerset, a vast commune covering two hundred acres and opulently built. At its heydey in 1850s it had more than a thousand inhabitants and its main tenet was unlicensed sexual intercourse. Name the person who set up this commune.

(a) Rev. Claire Wilson (b) Henry James Prince (c) Sir William Halstead (d) Montgomery Lion

28

ARTS AND ENTERTAINMENT

765. Which French novelist and poet became famous for his classic (and suppressed) novel of lesbianism called *Mademoiselle de Maupin*?

(a) Theophile Gautier (b) Emile Zola (c) Sacher-Masoch (d) Alexandre Dumas

766. He is best known for his novel *Couples* written in 1968, which marked a breakthrough in the literary treatment of sexual relationships. Who is he?

(a) D.H. Lawrence (b) William Faulkner (c) W.H. Auden (d) John Hoyer Updike

767. This American poet is best known for his *Leaves of Grass* which he first published in 1855. Most American critics condemned it as 'an indecent book' because of its overtly homosexual sentiments. Who was he?

(a) Washington Irving (b) James Fenimore Cooper (c) Walt Whitman (d) Henry Wadsworth Longfellow

768. Which Victorian prude edited *The Family Shakespeare* in 1818 removing those words and expressions which could not with propriety be read aloud in a family?

(a) Dr. Thomas Bowdler (b) Friedrich Schiller (c) James Fenimore Cooper (d) George Meredith

769. Which famous science writer, besides having written several science books, has also written *The Sensuous Dirty Old Man,* a book with an explicit sexual content?

(a) Arthur C. Clarke (b) J.R.R. Tolkien (c) J.G. Ballard (d) Isaac Asimov

770. This poet wrote a collection of songs, *The Merry Muses of Caledonia,* which contains his bawdiest lyrics. This collection was not published for the general public in uncensored form until 1965. Who is this poet?

(a) Lord Byron (b) Robert Burns (c) Percy Bysshe Shelley (d) William Wordsworth

771. Saint Gregory of Nazianzus, Bishop of Constantinople, ordered her books to be burned wherever they were found, because of their immoral content. He also termed her *gynaeon pornikon erotomanes* meaning that

she was a lewd nymphomaniac. Who was this famous female writer of antiquity?

(a) Sappho (b) Lesbia (c) Lucretia (d) Diana

772. This Latin poet was one of the most passionate love poets of the ancient world and wrote 25 poems to Lesbia, the woman he loved. Who was this famous poet?

(a) Sextus Propertius (b) Albius Tibullus (c) Homer (d) Gaius Valerius Catullus

773. Many of his stories are full of prostitutes, adultery, voyeurism and other sexual matters. He was also reported to be able to achieve an erection at will and to prove his virility he once took a witness to a brothel and had six girls in an hour. Who is this unique author?

(a) Guy de Maupassant (b) Marcel Proust (c) Jean-Paul Sartre (d) Albert Camus

774. This eccentric writer laced his works so heavily with vivid descriptions of sex and death that author Henry James labelled them 'vulgar'. Who was he?

(a) Albert Camus (b) William Faulkner (c) D.H. Lawrence (d) Gabriele D'Annunzio

775. Who wrote *Thy Neighbour's Wife,* which traced the evolution of American society from the prudery and restraints of the Victorian era to the libertine attitude of the present?

(a) Robert Ludlum (b) Irving Wallace (c) Gay Talese (d) Sidney Sheldon

776. Who wrote *Nôtre Dame des Fleurs,* an epic of transvestism and homosexuality?

(a) Jean Genet (b) Rudi Gernreich (c) Guy de Maupassant (d) Algernon Charles Swinburne

777. Which French publisher founded the Olympia Press in Paris in 1953 to print in English, authors banned in English-speaking countries?

(a) The Ghouls (b) Maurice Girodias (c) Sir Francis Dashwood (d) Mrs. Josephine Butler

778. Which Byzantine historian kept a secret record of the scandalous careers of Empress Theodora and her

friend Antonina, which was published posthumously as the *Secret History*?

(a) Procopius (b) Nicephorus (c) Alexius (d) Yolande

779. She was a famous sex symbol of her times. One volume of her autobiography is called *Goodness Has Nothing to Do With It.* Who is she?

(a) Clara Bow (b) Susann Langley (c) Mae West (d) Marlene Dietrich

780. Sperm to him meant emission of purest cerebral substance and therefore a loss of a potential act of artistic creation. Who was this famous author?

(a) Honoré de Balzac (b) Voltaire (c) George Bernard Shaw (d) Socrates

781. When this book was published in Italy in 1928, the British Home Secretary promptly ordered customs officials to prevent the import of any copies. The ban persisted until 1960. Which is the book?

(a) *Ulysses* (b) *Finnegans Wake* (c) *The Rainbow* (d) *Lady Chatterley's Lover*

782. This book was first published in 1955 in Paris after being turned down by a number of American publishers. It gained a certain reputation as a pornographic work describing the adventures of a middle-aged professor with a precociously nubile twelve-year-old girl, Dolores Haze. Which is the book?

(a) *Sons and Lovers* (b) *Ulysses* (c) *Lolita* (d) *Women in Love*

783. In which classical work would one find the following lines; "But her bosom, blessed be the Gods, is a living seduction. It bears twin breasts of the purity of ivory, rounded and that may be held within the five fingers of the hand"?

(a) *Ulysses* (b) *Arabian Nights* (c) *Sons and Lovers* (d) *Lolita*

784. When was a decree passed in England leading to a system of licensing all books before publication?

(a) AD 1138 (b) AD 1234 (c) AD 1470 (d) AD 1538

785. He was convicted of obscenity in 1727 for publishing *Venus in the Cloister,* and from his case derives the Anglo-American censorship law. Identify him.

(a) Edmund Curll (b) Léonor Fini (c) Alec Jeffreys (d) Basil Purdue

786. Title for title, he is the most successful novelist ever in English. His books notably eschew the love element. When asked about this in an interview he replied briskly, 'Sex? No time for it. Gets in the way of the action.' Identify the author.

(a) Frederick Forsyth (b) Harold Robbins (c) Alistair Maclean (d) Mickey Spillane

787. Who wrote *Ragionamenti* (Dialogues), a three-part lascivious conversation between an ex-whore and an ingénue about the sex lives of nuns, married women, and courtesans?

(a) John Cleland (b) Pietro Aretino (c) Felicien Rops (d) Margaret Sanger

788. Who wrote the book *Any Woman Can!* in 1972, which tried to popularize the extraordinary theory that the way to a man's heart was to feed him glasses of milk?

(a) Eric Berne (b) Sidney Smith (c) Anthony Busuttil (d) David Reuben

789. Havelock Ellis called his sixteen-volume autobiography a precious document for erotic psychology, and used many incidents from it to illustrate his own *Psychology of Sex.* Who was he?

(a) Nicolas Edmé Restif de la Bretonne (b) Casanova (c) John Wilmot, Earl of Rochester (d) William Thomas Stead

790. His most notorious work is a play called *Sodom or the Quintessence of Debauchery*, which opens with the king of Sodom, Bollixinon announcing, "With my prick I'll govern all the land". Who is the writer?

(a) Leonard Charles Smithers (b) Sir Charles Sedley (c) John Wilmot, Earl of Rochester (d) Edward Sellon

791. He was an explorer, swordsman, anthropologist and a formidable linguist speaking 25 languages. He worked for 14 years translating into English *The Perfumed Garden* from original Arabic, but on his death his wife Isabel destroyed the whole manuscript. Who was he?

(a) Samuel Butler (b) Sir Richard Francis Burton (c) Jonathan Swift (d) Winston Churchill

792. This French medieval poet of low life befriended pimps and prostitutes. His life in the medieval underworld of prostitutes is chronicled in two long poems, the *Testament* and the *Petit Testament.* Who is he?

(a) François Villon (b) Michel de Montaigne (c) François Rabelais (d) Trouvères

793. Who wrote the novel *The Ginger Man* noted for its explicit sexual content, the first unexpurgated edition of which could not appear in the U.K. before 1963?

(a) Henry de Montherlant (b) Anthony Burgess (c) J.P. Donleavy (d) Rex Warner

794. Who compiled *The Manual of Classical Erotology,* an anthology of extremely erotic passages from the works of Greek and Latin writers such as Virgil, Martial, Ovid, and Seneca?

(a) Len Deighton (b) Friedrich-Karl Forberg (c) Richard Burton (d) Max Muller

795. Who wrote *Satyricon,* a book with an explicit sexual content?

(a) Pliny, the Elder (b) Cato (c) Romulus (d) Petronius Arbiter

796. *Il piacere* (The Child of Pleasure, 1890) is one of the significant texts of European Decadence. Who wrote it?

(a) Gabriele d'Annunzio (b) Gèrard de Nerval (c) Émile Zola (d) Honoré de Balzac

797. This Latin poet and epigrammatist wrote a total of about 1,555 epigrams spread over twelve books. About 150 of them are still considered too obscene to translate. Who is he?

(a) Virgil (b) Seneca (c) Martial (d) Pliny, the Elder

798. In which novel by Marquis de Sade, written in 1791, does the heroine meet the pervert schoolmaster Rodin and four debauched monks who rape her and force her to perform fellatio?

(a) *Justine* (b) *Confessions of an Opium Eater* (c) *Visions of Sex* (d) *The Masochist*

799. Which poet wrote *Ars Amatoria* (The Art of Love) which has remained a classic sex manual till now?

(a) Sophocles (b) Ovid (c) Seneca (d) Virgil

800. Which French novelist, poet and pornographer usually wrote under the pen-name of Hugues Rebell?

(a) Marcel Proust (b) Henry de Montherlant (c) Andre Malraux (d) Georges Joseph Grassal

801. Which Latin writer, born in North Africa, in the second century A.D. wrote *The Golden Ass,* in which the hero Lucius is accidentally turned into an ass, and then copulates with a prostitute in the public amphitheatre?

(a) Pietro Aretino (b) Pliny the Elder (c) Lucius Apuleius (d) Seneca

802. Which American - Jewish homosexual poet is known for his poem *Howl,* which was unsuccessfully prosecuted in New York in 1961 for obscenity?

(a) Allen Ginsberg (b) William Schwenck Gilbert (c) Gary Snyder (d) Lawrence Ferlinghetti

803. Which British novelist wrote *The Well of Loneliness,* a book which was banned in Britain in 1928 and not reprinted until 1949?

(a) Christopher Hill (b) Radclyffe Hall (c) Robert Smythe Hichens (d) William Golding

804. Which story by Maupassant features the rare instance of adult breast-feeding?

(a) 'Idylle' (b) 'La Maison Tellier' (c) 'Miss Harriet' (d) 'Le Horla'

805. Which book by Steinbeck features adult breast-feeding?

(a) *Tortilla Flat* (b) *In Dubious Battle* (c) *The Winter of Our Discontent* (d) *The Grapes of Wrath*

806. Who is the author of *Sex and the Single Girl,* a milestone of the permissive society?

(a) Lenny Bruce (b) Mrs. Josephine Butler (c) Helen Gurley Brown (d) Sir Richard Burton

807. He was the last of the great artists of the rococo period, renowned for his erotic engravings for Restif

de la Bretonne's novel of lust and incest, *The Perverted Peasant.* Who was he?

(a) Giambattista Tiepolo (b) Francesco Guardi (c) Antonio Canaletto (d) Louis Binet

808. Who in 1968 organized the first international exhibition of erotic art?

(a) Phyllis Kronhausen (b) Eberhard Kronhausen (c) Filicien Rops (d) Wilhelmine Schroeder-Devrient

809. Where was the first international exhibition of erotic art shown?

(a) Paris (b) London (c) Lund (d) Aarhus

810. This French surrealist painter is best known for his obsessive portrayal of overglamorous nudes among funereal furnishings and tombs to produce an effect of moral anarchy. Who is or was he?

(a) Clovis Trouille (b) Marc Chagall (c) Salvador Dali (d) Max Ernst

811. Which erotic female cartoon-strip character, having huge breasts, was invented by a Russian underground organization called the PPP group?

(a) Catherina (b) Octobriana (c) Lind (d) Cutie

812. This painter once painted two pictures, entitled *Two Girls Disrobing for Their Bath* showing two sexy nude girls. When some art critics raised objections, he defended himself by saying, 'I assure you that I have placed the figures in a completely secluded spot so that they would not possibly encounter any observation from curious onlookers.' Who was this painter?

(a) Edgar Degas (b) Auguste Renoir (c) Eugène Delacroix (d) Léopold Robert

813. The Spanish painter Murillo (1617-82) was reprimanded by the Inquisition because

(a) he had shown Madonna with bare breasts (b) he had shown some animals copulating (c) he had shown Madonna with bare toes (d) he used to sleep with two wives at the same time

814. This Belgian artist specialized in erotic subjects, most notable of which are his winged phalli. He illustrated works by Baudelaire, de Sade, de Nerciat and Barbey d' Aurevilly. Who was he?

(a) Felicien Rops (b) Raoul Dufy (c) Domenichino (d) Luca della Robbia

815. This French painter and lithographer specialized in scenes of Parisian nightlife; his lively lithograph posters of performers at the Moulin Rouge Cabaret in Paris gave him enduring fame. Identify the painter.

(a) Edgar Degas (b) Auguste Renoir (c) Gustave Courbet (d) Henri de Toulouse-Lautrec

816. He was the supreme erotic illustrator and illustrated such works as *Fanny Hill*, *Stories from Aretino* and *The Thousand and One Nights*. Much of his work was privately printed, but in 1967 Gala Verlag of Hamburg published a two-volume limited edition of his drawings. Name him.

(a) Aubrey Beardsley (b) Marquis Franz von Bayros (c) Fragonard (d) Sir William Schwenck Gilbert

817. This film director was responsible for numerous explicitly sexual films that gave impetus to the European cinema in the late fifties. His works include *Summer with Monika,* and *Scenes from a Marriage.* Who is he?

(a) Sergei Eisenstein (b) Ingmar Bergman (c) Alexander Korda (d) John Grierson

818. Wagner based an opera on these legendary lovers. In his version of the story the couple drink some love-potion together and this scene is considered by many critics to be the most erotic piece of music ever written. Identify the lovers?

(a) Romeo and Juliet (b) Tristan and Isolde (c) Hero and Leander (d) Héloise and Abélard

819. Which erotic dance reputedly originating at the Moulin Rouge in Paris in the 1890s, led to the prosecution of the theatre's managers for indecencey?

(a) Twist (b) Rock 'n' Roll (c) Cancan (d) Cha cha cha

820. Sexual frustration of the bewildered adolescent was reflected in their early songs such as 'Please, Please Me', 'I Want to Hold Your Hand', 'She Loves You', and 'Can't Buy Me Love'. Identify them.

(a) The Beatles (b) The Yuppies (c) Lennon Brothers (d) The Gang of Four

821. Which famous Paris nightclub, founded in 1869, is directed by Michel Gyarmathy, a Hungarian refugee who selects the girls from candidates who undress in his office?

(a) Moulin Rouge (b) Les girls (c) Oui (d) Folies Bergère

822. Who, among the following, was one of the first recorded manufacturers of erotic pottery?

(a) Pliny the Elder (b) Seutonius (c) Marcus Perennius (d) Szabo

823. At twenty-seven in 1883, this British writer and womanizer was appointed editor of the *London Evening News*, reputedly after seducing the proprietor's wife. His editorial policy, according to his own admission, included only two subjects — fighting and sex (he used a four-letter word alliterating with fighting for the latter term). Who was he?

(a) Sir Richard Burton (b) Frank Harris (c) Leopold Sharkey (d) Oscar Wilde

824. Zerbinetta is a coquettish character in his opera *Ariadne auf Naxos*. So popular is this character that platenoid no. 693 is named after her. Who is the composer?

(a) Richard Strauss (b) Beethoven (c) Mozart (d) Chopin

825. Who wrote the opera *Die Liebe der Danaë*, based on the love story of Zeus and Danaë?

(a) Beethoven (b) Mozart (c) Chopin (d) Richard Strauss

826. Which Italian director is known for his two studies of Roman decadence, *La Dolce Vita* (1960) and *Satyricon* (1970), of which the former won a first prize at Cannes?

(a) Vittorio De Sica (b) Federico Fellini (c) Michelangelo Antonioni (d) Roberto Rossellini

29

EASY VIRTUE

827. Which celebrated English courtesan was born as Emma Crouch?

(a) Mata Hari (b) Cora Pearl (c) Brigitte Bardot (d) Bo Derek

828. Which glamour girl had red hair, pale beautiful skin and the motto that vice is seldom seen in rags?

(a) Cora Pearl (b) Marilyn Monroe (c) Anne Hathaway (d) Christine Keeler

829. Which Victorian courtesan was the mistress of Lord Cardigan for many years before marrying him on the death of his first wife?

(a) Kate Millet (b) Emma Stewart (c) Wilhelmine Schroeder Devrient (d) Adeline Horsey de Horsey

830. Which high class French courtesan was the mistress of Felix Faure, president of the French republic?

(a) Kate Millet (b) Marguerite Steinheil (c) Wilhelmine Schroeder Devrient (d) Richard Monckton Milnes

831. Which famous English courtesan was born as Amy Lyon?

(a) Lady Emma Hamilton (b) Lady Mary Ann Cotton (c) Her Higness Kitty Byron (d) Edith Thompson

832. Which famous English courtesan was the mistress of Lord Nelson?

(a) Lady Emma Hamilton (b) Lady Margaret Allen (c) Gabrielle Bompard (d) Charlotte Bryant

833. This famous prostitute, formerly a Belfast shop-assistant, became known as the Queen of Whoredom after she had relieved General H.R.H. Prince Jung Bahadur of £ 250,000 for a one-night session. Who was she?

(a) Skittles (b) Cora Pearl (c) Laura Bell (d) Bo Derek

834. Who are or were the horsebreakers?

(a) A group of horsemen who used to bring customers to the red light areas (b) A select group of society courtesans in London in the 1860s (c) A group of courtesans in Germany who provided 'free service' on Fridays (d) Prostitutes with a Ph.D. degree.

835. What was the name given to ancient Greek prostitutes of the highest class?

(a) Concubines (b) Whores (c) Geisha (d) Hetaerae

836. Who was the mistress of Pericles, who was also blamed for starting the wars against Sparta?

(a) Aspasia (b) Hyxodon (c) Xeno (d) Thais

837. Which famous courtesan accompanied Alexander the Great on his campaigns and later married king Ptolemy of Egypt?

(a) Hypatia (b) Aspasia (c) Thais (d) Xeno

838. One of Julius Caesar's mistresses was the mother of Marcus Junius Brutus. Who was she?

(a) Servilia (b) Julia (c) Tatiana (d) Tertia

839. Devadasis are temple prostitutes in India, who are given to the temple before puberty. In which Indian state is this tradition still continuing?

(a) Assam (b) Rajasthan (c) Himachal Pradesh (d) Karnataka

840. Devadasis believe themselves to be lawfully married to a goddess. Which one?

(a) Durga (b) Vaishno Devi (c) Yellamma (d) Kali

841. According to tradition, who brought the first devadasis to their goddess for worship?

(a) Parasurama (b) Indra (c) Kuber (d) Mithilesh

842. Before Devadasis are inducted into temple service, some white beads are tied to their body, which marks their formal induction into the devadasi group. What are these heads called?

(a) Units (b) *Tali* (c) *Chabi* (d) *Dana*

843. Who was Napolean's mistress during his Egyptian Campaign of 1798?

(a) Pauline Fourès (b) Mademoiselle de Montansier (c) Madame Permon (d) Marguérite Weymer

844. In ancient India, offering of a girl to the temple to serve as a devadasi was considered sacred. Which religious book says that the one who would offer a girl to a temple would attain *suryalok*?

(a) *Samveda* (b) *Atharvaveda* (c) *Garuda Puran* (d) *Bhavishya Puran*

845. Which people offer their first or sometimes the fifth daughter to the temple?

(a) Bhils (b) Santhals (c) Gonds (d) Koriyos

846. While still in her teens she was known for her insatiability. One of her erotic specialities was to lie on the floor and have barley strewn on her vulva so that trained geese could come and pick the grains off. Who was she?

(a) Mata Hari (b) Theodora (c) Belle Boyd (d) Natalie Barney

847. Who was the first known madam or female proprietor of a house of prostitution?

(a) Hung Yai (b) Cora Pearl (c) Aspasia (d) Hypatia

848. She was the most famous of Roman concubines and left a vast estate gleaned from her sexual trafficking with Roman aristocrats. According to her will most of her wealth was to be spent on lavish festivals in honour of the goddess Flora. Who was she?

(a) Julia (b) Hypatia (c) Flora (d) Aspasia

849. Which Roman emperor decreed that Roman prostitutes could no longer travel in public on litters?

(a) Hadrian (b) Gallus (c) Maximinus (d) Domitian

850. Which Holy Roman Emperor became so enraged at the usual practice of Crusaders taking whores with them on their voyages that he ordered all soldiers whipped if caught with a prostitute and decreed that the latter's nose be sliced off?

(a) Frederick Barbarossa (b) Lothair II (c) Heinrich II, the Saint (d) Heinrich III, the Black

851. Which King laid down the first severe laws against prostitution in Europe?

(a) Robert II, the Pious (b) Guido of Spoleto (c) King Alfonso IX of Castile (d) Otto I, the Great

852. This French king decided to curb prostitution by making very stringent laws. But he was forced to modify his edict to less drastic regulations when because of the unavailability of prostitutes decent

women began to be raped by ruffians. Who was this king?

(a) Hugh Capet (b) Louis IX (c) Philip III, the Bold (d) Charles IV

853. Which famous English prostitute threw the Duke of York out of bed when he gave her just £ 50 as her fees, instead of her usual £ 100?

(a) Kitty Fisher (b) Ninon de Lenclos (c) Natalie Barney (d) Belle Boyd

854. Who was referred to as a whore with 'a sewer of a mouth'?

(a) La Belle Otero (b) Harriette Wilson (c) Adah Isaacs Menken (d) Cora Pearl

855. Which famous Greek courtesan was stoned to death?

(a) Rhodopis (b) Habrotonon (c) Lais (d) Timandra

856. Which famous Greek courtesan was the mistress of the great Athenian sculptor Praxiteles, who also used her as a model for his statues of Aphrodite?

(a) Theodote (b) Hera (c) Timandra (d) Phryne

857. Which famous Greek courtesan amassed so much wealth that she built one of the Egyptian pyramids at her own expense?

(a) Rhodopis (b) Myrrhina (c) Aristagora (d) Phila

858. After the philospher Aristotle's wife Pythias died, he is said to have lived with a prostitute. Which one?

(a) Myrrhina (b) Herpyllis (c) Phila (d) Nicosia

859. What were the highest class of prostitutes called in ancient Rome?

(a) Famosae (b) Hetaerae (c) Lupae (d) Delicatae

860. There are many references to concubines in the Old Testament. How many concubines did David have?

(a) 2 (b) 10 (c) 17 (d) 101

861. How many concubines did Solomon have?

(a) 300 (b) 500 (c) 1001 (d) 10,001

862. And finally, how many concubines did Rehoboam have?

(a) 40 (b) 50 (c) 60 (d) 71

863. Which famous Greek courtesan derived her name from her rosy face?

(a) Rhodopis (b) Theodote (c) Habrotonon (d) Lais

864. In ancient Rome, daughters of respectable families followed the calling of prostitution either because they needed the money or because they enjoyed the pleasure. What were these prostitutes called?

(a) Fornices (b) Doris (c) Lupae (d) Famosae

865. Some prostitutes in ancient Rome lived in squalid shelters in the woods or in abandoned or ruined buildings and entertained their customers in the alley-ways or even in the less frequented streets. What were these prostitutes called?

(a) Gallinae (b) Lupae (c) Diabolares (d) Quadrantariae

866. In ancient Rome, there were some bakers' girls or slaves, who were sent out to sell little cakes of the shapes of the genital organs of men or women for sacrificial offerings, but they carried on the business of prostitution as a side-line. What were these prostitutes called?

(a) Copae (b) Gallinae (c) Elicariae (d) Noctiliae

867. They had their homes in Roman cemeteries, where they worked as professional mourners, but as a side-business, they also indulged in prostitution. What were these prostitutes of ancient Rome called?

(a) Bustuariae (b) Copae (c) Noctiliae (d) Vixae

868. Slave girls, chambermaids, etc., in Roman taverns and inns, who could be hired by the guests as bed mates for the night were called

(a) diabolares (b) tavernae (c) vixae (d) copae

869. Ancient Rome had a class of prostitutes who prowled the streets at night looking for customers like our own night-walkers. These prostitutes were called

(a) gallinae (b) noctiliae (c) doris (d) forariae

870. These Roman prostitutes were quite degraded and usually drunk. What were they known as?

(a) Alcoholae (b) Vixae (c) Blitidae (d) Tavernae

871. In ancient Rome what or who were the *diabolares*?

(a) Prostitutes who killed their customers (b) Prostitutes who charged a fee of one diabolon (c) Ugly prostitutes (d) Prostitutes who were thieves also

872. Country girls who solicited their customers at the roadsides were called

(a) roadae (b) vixae (c) forariae (d) gallinae

873. These Roman prostitutes were also petty thieves. What were they called?

(a) Gallinae (b) Vixae (c) Dacoitae (d) Quadrantariae

874. These Roman prostitutes would sleep with someone for the smallest copper coin made in Rome or even for bread, drink or a piece of fish. They were known as

(a) pettiae (b) quadrantariae (c) vixae (d) philiae

875. In which ancient civilization every woman had to prostitute herself at least once in her life?

(a) Etruscans (b) Scythians (c) Huns (d) Babylonians

876. When a former mistress threatened to publish her diary and letters, the Duke of Wellington made this famous remark, 'Publish and be damned'. Identify this mischievous mistress.

(a) Kitty Fisher (b) Cora Pearl (c) Harriette Wilson (d) Billie Holliday

877. She was a London brothel keeper of the late eighteenth century. One of her books that has survived is a collection of bawdy stories called *The Voluptuarian Cabinet* (1777). Who is she?

(a) Eshma Dashwood (b) Mrs. Mary Wilson (c) Henrietta Haigh (d) Countess of Rochester

878. At a sea festival for Aphrodite and Poseidon, this celebrated Greek courtesan stripped at the temple, walked naked through the crowds down to the sheashore, and dived into the waves. On her reemergence she was acclaimed as the reincarnation of seaborn Aphrodite. Who was this courtesan?

(a) Phryne (b) Diabolares (c) Lais (d) Rhodopis

879. For the above indecency, this Greek courtesan was brought to trial. Who was her counsel?

(a) Socrates (b) Plato (c) Hypereides (d) Aristotle

880. Intrigue and adultery by concubines in medieval Sultan's harems were punished by drowning the women in weighted sacks. One particularly cruel seventeenth century Sultan is reputed to have drowned as many as three hundred concubines in a single occasion. Who is he?

(a) Aurangzeb (b) Mohammad Shah 'Rangila' (c) Daswant (d) Ibrahim

881. Who wrote *Prostitution and Society* (1962), a three-volume historical survey of prostitution?

(a) Fernando Henriques (b) Elizabeth Bowen (c) Nevil Shute (d) Normal Mailer

882. Quite surprisingly one of the platenoids is named after a Greek courtesan. Who is she?

(a) Rhodopis (b) Aspasia (c) Habrotonon (d) Lais

883. Which Egyptian Pharaoh placed his own daughter in a brothel in order to lay hands on a clever thief who had been robbing him?

(a) Zozer (b) Tutankhamen (c) Ramesses II (d) Rhampsinitus

884. The French writer Guy de Maupassant had a sympathy for prostitutes. In which of his works are prostitutes sympathetically portrayed?

(a) *La Maison Tellier* (b) *Boule de Suif* (c) *Une Vie* (d) *Bel-Ami*

885. What are the brothel areas in Tokyo known as?

(a) Shami-Ze (b) Yohasina (c) Yoshiwara (d) Ban-lasan

886. In ancient Babylon who were the *zermashitu*?

(a) Temple prostitutes (b) Virgins (c) Females who married more than one male (d) Prostitutes who exclusively provided oral sex

887. Skittles was the nickname of the most famous of the fashionable and expensive Victorian whores. Who was she?

(a) Kitty Fischer (b) Catherine Walters (c) Natalie Barney (d) Rosa Benheur

888. In which late seventeenth-century London club lectures were given on the finer points of prostitution?

(a) The Courtesan (b) The Hetairai (c) The Club of Seven Sisters (d) Beaux's Club

889. This beautiful Victorian widow and ex-prostitute owned a string of high-class brothels. Prince of Wales was believed to be one of her clients. She was prosecuted in 1885 and fined two hundred pounds and she paid the fine in cash before leaving the court. Who was she?

(a) Kitty Fisher (b) Charlotte Hayes (c) Mrs. Mary Jeffries (d) Valentino Latvio

890. What are the prophylactoria?

(a) Reform homes in certain communist countries such as China where prostitutes are rehabilitated (b) A drug kit officially distributed to prostitutes in certain countries to help prophylaxis against venereal diseases (c) A collective name for sex-aids used by prostitutes (d) Barrier contraceptives supplied to customers by high class prostitutes, so that venereal diseases don't spread.

891. By the Wolfenden Report in 1957, prostitution was effectively cleared off the streets of which country?

(a) Canada (b) U.K. (c) U.S.A. (d) West Germany

892. They are supposed to be the most beautiful male prostitutes in the world, living near the Vatican, Rome. Prices for 'quick times' are 10,000 lira — twice the fee for female prostitutes living nearby. What are they known as?

(a) Copulati (b) Fenneli (c) Starkies (d) Bangers

893. This Victorian brothel owner was called 'the queen of her profession'. When she opened her 'house of flagellation' at 28 Charlotte Street, London, in 1828, she announced the invention of the Berkely horse — a flagellation machine meant for masochistic clients. Who was she?

(a) Mrs. Theresa Berkely (b) Valentino Latvia (c) Kitty Fischer (d) Big Bertha

30

POTPOURRI

894. Feminine beauty is more a subjective feeling rather than an objective thing. Yet, a unit to measure feminine beauty has been suggested. What is it?

     (a) Beautimetre (b) Attractivon (c) Millihelen (d) No such absurd suggestion has been made

895. Who staged the earliest international beauty contest?

     (a) P.T. Barnum (b) Thomas Topham (c) Will Kemp (d) William McGonagall

896. Who is the only Indian woman to have won the Miss World Contest?

     (a) Zeenat Aman (b) Rita Faria (c) Swaroop Sampat (d) Hema Malini

897. When was the earliest international beauty contest organized?

     (a) June 1855 (b) January 1871 (c) December 1899 (d) July 1921

898. When was the earliest Miss America Contest staged?

     (a) 1919 (b) 1931 (c) 1943 (d) 1921

899. Who won the first Miss America Contest?

     (a) Margaret Gorman (b) Mary Jeffries (c) Adeline Horsey (d) Mata Hari

900. When did the annual Miss World Contest begin?

     (a) January 1921 (b) February 1931 (c) June 1941 (d) July 1951

901. When did the annual Miss Universe Contest begin?

     (a) 1945 (b) 1952 (c) 1957 (d) 1962

902. A stage in infantile sexual development when the child falls in love with his mother is called

     (a) mother complex (b) love-mum complex (c) Oedipus complex (d) Electra complex

903. A stage in infantile sexual development when a young girl falls in love with her father is known as

     (a) Lear complex (b) Electra complex (c) girl complex (d) father fixation

904. Jocasta complex is the morbid attachment between

(a) mother and son (b) brother and sister (c) grandfather and granddaughter (d) no such complex is known

905. Lear complex is a case of marked attachment between

(a) two brothers (b) two sisters (c) father and daughter (d) brother and sister

906. Diana complex refers to

(a) marked attachment to a neighbour's daughter (b) making love to neighbour's wife (c) making love to one's teacher (d) masculine tendencies in the female

907. What is a 'double entendre'?

(a) A girl who provides sexual pleasure in the absence of wife (b) Making love to wife in abnormal positions (c) A word having double meaning, one of which is generally sexual in nature (d) Sex play with two women at the same time

908. What was the fourteenth-century religious order whose monks and nuns were obliged to live in the same monastery but without having sexual intercourse?

(a) Order of Birgitta (b) Order of Calvins (c) Johnies (d) Protestants

909. What is or was a 'bigg'?

(a) A sexy woman (b) Extra nipple in a woman (c) A juicy lip (d) A sexy man

910. A survey of childless women was conducted in Texas, which attempted to relate the size of breasts with the I.Q. of women. According to this survey, women having bigger breasts had

(a) a greater IQ (b) a lesser IQ (c) no relationship was found (d) an IQ of less than 50

911. The name of which plant comes from a Greek word meaning testicle?

(a) Orchid (b) Willow (c) Palm (d) Yam

912. Which sacred plant of the Druids confers the right of a kiss if a woman is caught standing under it?

(a) Orchid (b) Mistletoe (c) Palm (d) Yam

913. According to tradition and folklore, the sprigs of this plant placed under a girl's pillow would enable her to dream of her future husband. Name it.

(a) Willow (b) Oak (c) Rosemary (d) Yew

914. In demonology, what is the name given to a male demon who has sexual intercourse with sleeping women?

(a) Incubus (b) Succubus (c) Concubus (d) Busbus

915. And what is the name given to a female demon who has intercourse with men?

(a) Jade (b) Succubus (c) Concubus (d) Busbus

916. Who is a Mohel?

(a) A person who procures customers for prostitutes (b) A person who is infected with syphilis (c) Jewish ritual surgeon who performs circumcisions on eight-day-old boys (d) A Mayan priest who approved marriages among the tribals

917. Who helped found the Proclamation Society, later titled the Society for the Suppression of Vice, to stamp out blasphemy and obscenity and rescue 'fallen women'?

(a) Carl Gustav Jung (b) Dr Thomas Bowdler (c) Marcus Perennius (d) Arbiter Petronius

918. The word for the female organ vagina quite understandably has a feminine gender in all languages, but one. Which language?

(a) Swedish (b) German (c) French (d) Portuguese

919. Which well-known act was done to impress Hollywood actress Jodie Foster?

(a) Mark Lindbergh crossing the Niagra falls (b) Harry Houdini diving from Eiffel Towel (c) John Hinkley trying to assassinate Ronald Reagan (d) Harold Macmillan passing on British secrets to China

920. Who are or were the 'khawals'?

(a) Egyptian transvestite male dancers-cum-prostitutes (b) Priests who solemnize marriages in Egypt (c) Marriage guests who bring expensive presents in weddings (d) Friends of the bridegroom who participate in all ceremonies in Egyptian marriages

921. In which year did the Egyptian government prohibit female public dancers and prostitutes?

(a) 1707 (b) 1834 (c) 1896 (d) 1936

922. An inflatable life jacket, that was issued to airmen in the Second World War, was named after a well-known sex symbol. Who was she?

(a) Briggitte Bardot (b) Raquel Welch (c) Marilyn Monroe (d) Mae West

923. Which book did the erotic movie star Linda Lovelace write, which was published by Pinnacle Books in 1973?

(a) *Inside Linda Lovelace* (b) *Sex and My Life* (c) *The Pleasure of Sex* (d) *My Husband and Sex*

924. Where was the first World Sex Fair held?

(a) Paris (b) Rome (c) Copenhagen (d) New York

925. And when was it held?

(a) January 1901 (b) August 1941 (c) September 1963 (d) October 1969

926. Where was the second World Sex Fair held?

(a) Odense (b) Michigan (c) Bonn (d) Vienna

927. And when was it held?

(a) March 1970 (b) October 1970 (c) October 1971 (d) January 1973

928. Which secretary and special agent of the New York Society for the Suppression of Vice made a law in 1873, which forbade the distribution of obscene matter through the U.S. mail?

(a) Frank Harris (b) Anthony Comstock (c) Alex Comfort (d) John Napier

929. Who in 1905 coined the word Comstockery to describe a narrow moralistic censorship?

(a) James Joyce (b) E.M. Forster (c) Joseph Conrad (d) George Bernard Shaw

930. In 1972, his one-inch penis was offered for sale at Christies but failed to reach the reserve price. Who was this famous man?

(a) Percy Bysshe Shelley (b) Henry VIII (c) Napoleon Bonaparte (d) Louis XIV

931. He had his wife's lover executed and his head put in a jar of alcohol. She had to keep the jar in her bedroom. Who was this tyrant?

(a) Caligula (b) Peter the Great (c) Czar Nicholas III (d) Nero

932. When his favourite wife Mumtaz Mahal died, giving birth to a child, Shahjehan ordered Taj Mahal to be built as a memorial. Which child was it?

(a) Her first child (b) Her third child (c) Her ninth child (d) Her fourteenth child

933. In July 1813 this famous man seduced his married half-sister, Augusta Leigh. Who was he?

(a) Lord Byron (b) Franz Liszt (c) Percy Bysshe Shelley (d) Robert Burns

934. The word Onanism is a synonym of

(a) anal intercourse (b) oral intercourse (c) masturbation (d) intercourse in water

935. A method of contraception used by certain couples is withdrawal of the male organ just before emission. This method of sexual intercourse is known as

(a) coitus reservatus (b) coitus interruptus (c) coitus obstructs (d) coitus finitus

936. *Coitus ã la Vache* is a term meaning

(a) masturbation (b) coitus with a horse (c) coitus with a statue (d) coitus from behind

937. The term coitus comes from

(a) an Egyptian word meaning love (b) a Greek word meaning caressing (c) a Latin word meaning to come together (d) a Latin word meaning indecency

938. A method of birth control in which the base of the male organ is gripped tightly between finger and thumb at the moment of ejaculation is known as

(a) coitus obstructus (b) karezza (c) oneida method (d) zugassánt

939. Sexual intercourse in which the male withholds his orgasm as a means of contraception is known as

(a) coitus reservatus (b) karezza (c) zugassant (d) all of the above

940. The term masturbation comes from two Latin words meaning

(a) obscene activity (b) defilement by hand (c) unnatural intercourse (d) sinful activity

941. Which was the first important printed attack on masturbation?

(a) *Defilement by Hand* by Vesalius (b) *A Treatise on Manustupration* by Hippocrates (c) *Onania, the Heinous Sin of Self-pollution* by Bekker (d) *The Disease of the Insane* by Oliver Wendell Holmes

942. She once entered a club and purposefully unbuttoning her blouse, displayed her surgically enhanced bosom to the pop-eyed diners and said, 'Darlings, do you like my new breasts? I've just had them done—aren't they marvellous'?

(a) Mae West (b) Tallulah Bankhead (c) Marlene Dietrich (d) Protima Bedi

943. She rode through the streets of Coventry completely naked on horseback, in order to get the taxes on people reduced. Who was she?

(a) Nancy Astor (b) Mata Hari (c) Lady Godiva (d) Emma Toilette

944. Egyptian god Osiris was killed by his brother Set treacherously in order to usurp the throne. How does his wife Isis revive him?

(a) By incantations to the god of love (b) By massaging his body with magical potion (c) By asking the goddess of sexual intercourse to infuse life in him (d) By sucking his penis

945. In Greek mythology who severed his father's genitalia with a flint sickle?

(a) Cronus (b) Pegasus (c) Bellerophon (d) Hercules

946. On his marriage night, when he was engaged in vigorous intercourse with his wife, her pet pug, Fortuné, thinking that he was attacking his mistress, bit him on his bare left calf, thus ruining the pleasures of his first night. Who was he?

(a) Groucho Marx (b) Napoleon Bonaparte (c) Karl Marx (d) Leon Trotsky

947. In which film was a fake cock made out of pork sausage for a castration scene?

(a) *Caligula* (b) *The Death Trap* (c) *Mickey Mouse* (d) *You're in the Army Now*

948. Which famous philosopher propounded the theory of tetragamy which advocated that two men shared a woman as a wife until she was past childbearing age, whereupon they should marry a second young woman, whilst continuing to care for their first wife?

(a) Jean-Paul Sartre (b) Sigmund Freud (c) Immanuel Kant (d) Arthur Schopenhauer

949. There is a long tradition that sometimes a couple can get inseparably locked in sexual intercourse through swelling of penis. What is the medical name given to such a term?

(a) *Penis Aculeatus* (b) *Penis Urethratus* (c) *Penis Captivus* (d) *Tentorialism*

950. There is a long tradition among certain tribes, especially the Naga of Manipur, Gond of Mandla, primitive Lohar of Raipur and Baiga that certain nubile girls have teeth in their vagina and if someone tries to rape them, they can cut off the male organ with those teeth. What is this condition called?

(a) *Infantile vagina* (b) Demonical vagina (c) *Vagina horriblia* (d) *Vagina dentata*

951. There is a long tradition among certain tribes that the male organ may contain teeth which may injure the vagina upon intercourse. What is this condition called?

(a) *Penis aculeatus* (b) *Penis urethratus* (c) *Penis damselivas* (d) *Penis injurious*

952. Who is reputed to have written the longest love letter?

(a) Sonali Dasgupta (b) Lady Mountbatten (c) Marcel de Leclure (d) Romeo

953. She performed this famous striptease act at the Palace music hall in 1911. It was called the Dance of the Bee and newspapers reported that it consisted of 'the lady pretending that a bee has crawled into her clothes, and madly snatching them off!' Who was this striptease dancer?

(a) Mata Hari (b) Belle Boyd (c) Natalie Barney (d) Stasia Napierkowska

954. Which Avant-garde American dress designer became famous for the sheer nylon 'no-bra bra,' now a fairly common item of female lingerie?

(a) Rudi Gernreich (b) Jean Genet (c) Henry Mill (d) Albert Ellis

955. What is a *godemichet*?

(a) A whore who specializes in oral sex (b) The custom of walking naked on streets (c) A person who performs sex with his close relatives (d) A highly sophisticated form of dildo, usually made of solid glass

956. What does the technical term 'the Coolidge effect' mean?

(a) Wasting of body by excessive sexual intercourse (b) Re-arousal of a male animal by a new female (c) Conversion of a male to a female by hormonal treatment (d) Treatment of a psychiatric patient by severing his testes

957. What is known as Croupade?

(a) A group of positions for sexual intercourse involving entry of the penis into a woman's vagina from behind (b) Beating of drums at the time of the birth of a double-headed monster, signifying that God has visited (c) Sexual orgies among marriage guests on the wedding night (d) The custom of two brothers marrying two sisters simultaneously

958. What is cruising?

(a) Having sex in a boat (b) Having sex in an aeroplane (c) Seeking a partner for sexual act (d) Beating one's mother to get sexual pleasure

959. What is described by the old Latin term *figura veneris prima*?

(a) A position of sexual intercourse in which the man lies on top (b) Sexual intercourse with a beast (c) Sexual intercourse with a statue (d) Sexual intercourse in which the woman lies on top

960. Which English word is derived from a Greek word meaning 'being nude'?

(a) Exhibit (b) Coitus (c) Caress (d) Gymnasium

961. What is the oceanic position?

(a) Making love in an ocean (b) Making love on an isolated island (c) A coital position in which the woman lies on her back with the man squatting or kneeling between her spread legs (d) A strange coital position in which partners come together much like sea animals having sexual intercourse

962. Sarmassation means

(a) stopping sexual activity suddenly (b) amorous caressing of female flesh (c) making love to an animal (d) making love to an old woman

963. He was the most outrageous rake. In 1631 he was tried for forcing his daughter to sleep with a servant called Skipwith. Who was he?

(a) Lord Castlehaven (b) Sir Francis Dashwood (c) Don Juan (d) Casanova

964. Which of the Ten Commandments prohibits adultery?

(a) 1st (b) 3rd (c) 7th (d) 10th

965. A girl with dimples in her cheeks is supposed to be sexually more attractive. According to tradition what are these dimples caused by?

(a) Too much laughing in the previous incarnation (b) Being the seventh daughter in the family (c) Being the only daughter in the family (d) Angel's kisses

966. Which famous Greek courtesan's name was derived from her toad like complexion?

(a) Lais (b) Timandra (c) Phryne (d) Rhodopis

967. Who are or were the Castrati?

(a) People with enlarged testes (b) People whose testes are removed before puberty (c) People who lack testes congenitally (d) Women who have a pair of testes

968. A fear of being deprived of the male sexual organs is called

(a) Zeus Complex (b) Andromeda Complex (c) Abelard Complex (d) Castration Complex

969. What is or was the *Index Librorum Prohibitorum*?

(a) A list of banned books (b) A list of prostitutes having venereal disease (c) A list of sexual criminals (d) A list of nubile virgins

970. When was the *Index Librorum Prohibitorum* issued?

(a) 1564 (b) 1662 (c) 1701 (d) 1843

971. Of all European countries from the seventeenth to the nineteenth centuries, only one country allowed virtual press freedom. Name it.

(a) France (b) Germany (c) Italy (d) Holland

972. What are or were the merkins?

(a) Small boys used in seventeenth century England for pederasty (b) Dildoes made of prime ivory (c) Toupees for the pudenda (d) Artificial breasts made from pig's fat in eighteenth century France

973. When he died of his excesses, at the age of thirty-three, he asked his executors to burn all his 'profane and lewd writings'. Who was he?

(a) John Wilmot, Earl of Rochester (b) David Reuben (c) Marquis de Sade (d) Leopold von Sacher-Masoch

974. The word pornography comes from

(a) a Latin root meaning nude photography (b) a Greek root meaning writing about harlots (c) a Greek root meaning obscene actions (d) a Latin root meaning titillation by writing or drawing

975. When Lady Godiva was riding naked on horseback on the streets of Coventry, everyone graciously remained indoors. One person however decided to take advantage of this situation and actually saw her naked. Who was he?

(a) Her erstwhile lover (b) Peeping Tom (c) A paralytic bachelor who had never seen a naked lady before (d) A curious eight-year-old child

976. When he wrote to the poet Horace, he used to address him as *purissimum penem* — "my most illustrious penis." Who was he?

(a) Tiberius (b) Caligula (c) Claudius (d) Augustus

977. Sexual caresses short of intercourse are known as

(a) petting (b) wetting (c) stroking (d) fingering

978. Where was the 1st International Conference on Orgasm 1991 held?

(a) Chicago (b) Paris (c) New Delhi (d) Hong Kong

979. Because of the growing cynicism regarding the nudist movement, in 1961 the British Sunbathing Association resolved to ban the word *nudism*. Which word was used in place of this?

(a) Liberalism (b) Naturism (c) Hellenism (d) Primitivism

980. Which Roman emperor had to banish his daughter to a tiny island because she had become a whore?

(a) Augustus (b) Hadrian (c) Marcus Aurelius (d) Caracalla

981. How many Calories does one lose in an average sex act?

(a) 50 (b) 200 (c) 1,000 (d) 1,200

982. What is or was the Hays Office Code?

(a) An elaborate set of rules formulated by Vincent Hays to prevent sexual harassment of girls in offices (b) A secret code which London police kept, detailing addresses of all prostitutes with venereal diseases (c) A list of homosexual murderers maintained by the British Home Office (d) Film censorship formula operating in the U.S. from 1930 to 1966

983. Which internationally noted charitable trust was founded in 1958 in London for research into sexual problems?

(a) The Educator (b) Albany Trust (c) Zed Trust (d) Pinkerton

31
PICTURE QUIZ

Photographs after p. 132

984. What does this picture show?
985. He is a pioneer in sex research. Who is he?
986. What is this strange looking contraption?
987. What is this strange looking contraption?

988. Which scientific instrument is this?

989. What is this instrument?

990. Which famous artist is known for such typical painting style, which among other things portrays voluptuousness and sexuality?

991. What is this strange looking contraption?

992. His name equals Don Juan's as a synonym for a promiscuous womanizer. His speciality was seducing his friends' wives and daughters often two at a time. Who is he?

993. Who is this buxom lady?

994. Who is this sexy looking woman?

995. Who is this buxom lady?

996. Who is this sexy lady?

997. Who is this woman?

998. Who is this smiling lady?

999. What is this figure showing?

1000. Who is this person?

984

985

986

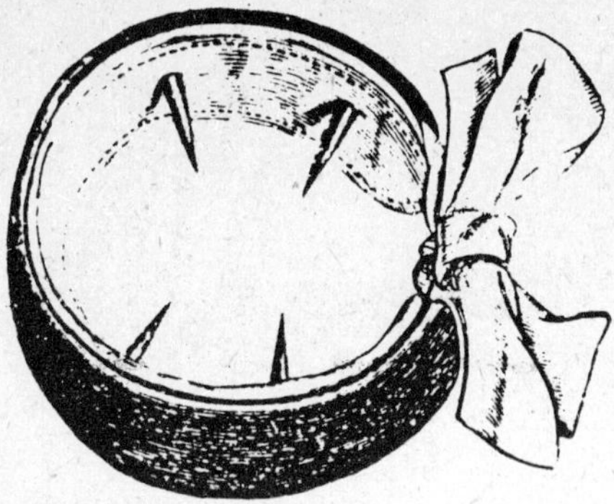

987

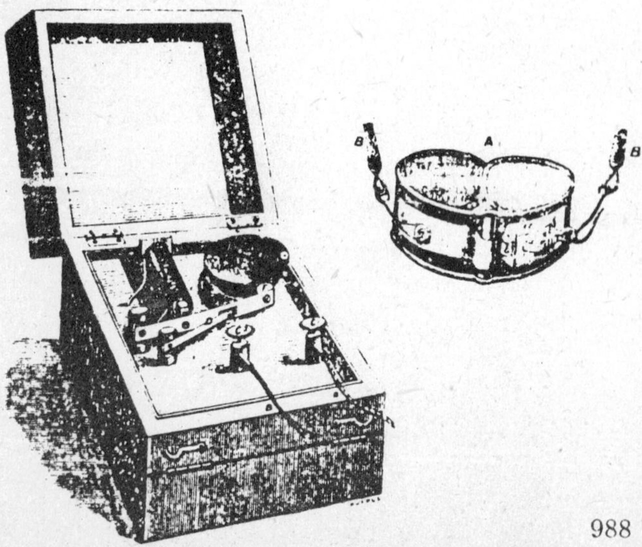

988

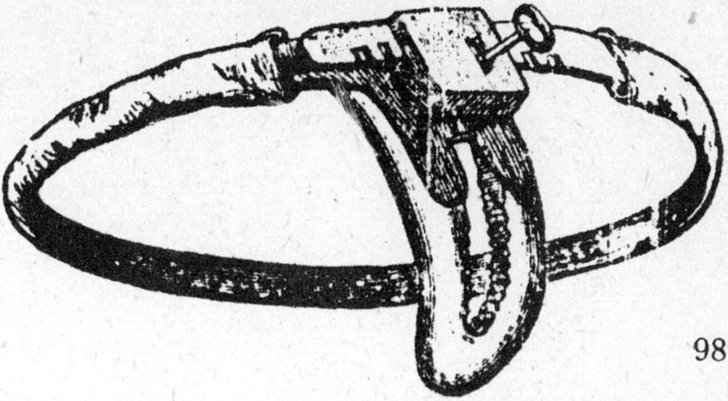

989

990

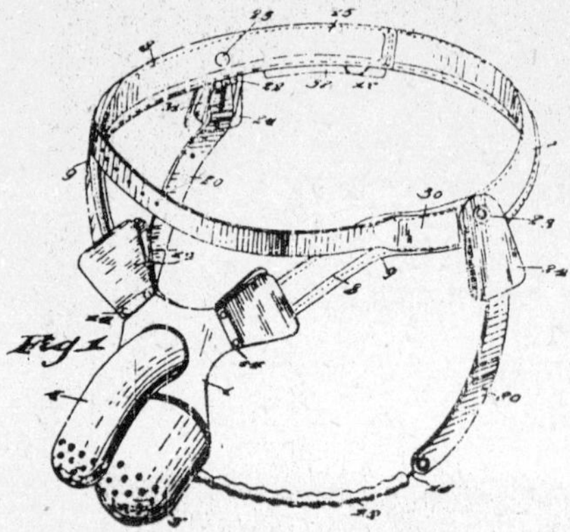

991

992

993

994

995

996

997

998

999

1000

32

BONUS

1001. Here you will find an array of different ways of saying 'I love you', in different languages. Go through them carefully and identify the language (You can even use them in greeting cards, in case you hesitate to say so in clear English to your friend).

a. Afekrishalehou
b. Ana b'hibbik
c. Bon sro lanh oon
d. Wo ai ni
e. Jeg elsker Dig
f. Ik houd van je
g. Tora dust midaram
h. Minä rakistan sinua
i. Je t'aime
j. Tá grá agam ort
k. Ich liebe dich
l. S'agapó
m. Ina sonki
n. Ani ohev otakh
o. Nu'umi unangwa'ta
p. Szeretlek
q. Saja kasih saudari
r. Ti voglio bene
s. Watakushi-wa anata-wo aishimasu
t. Tangsinũl sarang hä yo
u. Khoi huk chau
v. Nalingi yo
w. Konoronhkwa
x. Ayór ánósh'ní
y. Jeg elsker Dem
z. Ja ciç kocham

aa. Te inbesc
bb. Ya tebya liubliu
cc. Techíhhila
dd. Te quiero
ee. Ninikupenda
ff. Jag älska Dig
gg. Chăn ráte khun
hh. Ben sevi seviyorum
ii. Tôi yêu em
jj. Yr wyf yn du garu
kk. Tom ho' ichema

ANSWERS

1. (c) Solon passed these laws sometime between 600 B.C. and 500 B.C.
2. (d)
3. (a)
4. (c) It contains a drug called atropine, which dilates the pupils of the eyes and thus make them look larger and more attractive. In fact, another name for this plant is Belladonna which comes from Italian words "bella" or beautiful and "donna" or lady.
5. (d)
6. (a) Tissot (1728-97) wrote this book in 1766, which later became very influential.
7. (b) This society had their own publication, *Journal of Orificial Surgery*.
8. (d)
9. (c) After the birth of a son, this period was merely 33 days.
10. (a)
11. (d)
12. (b) According to legend Lycurgus was the promulgator of Spartan laws.
13. (a) Arches are "fornices" in Latin.
14. (c)
15. (a) Like most other Romans he was a homosexual. So common was the practice of anal intercourse in ancient Rome that one contemporary writer cited this activity as the major cause of hemorrhoids!
16. (a)
17. (c)
18. (a) The position is now frequently known as the missionary position.
19. (d) The members of this club included such prominent figures as the politician John Wilkes, the

novelist Lawrence Sterne, the diarist Horace Walpole, the wit George Selwyn, and the Chevalier d'Eon!

20. (b) In his Epistle to the Corinthians he goes to the extent of saying, 'It is good for a man not to touch a woman'.
21. (d) The plant was said to shriek if uprooted and those who heard it became insane. For this reason whoever wanted to uproot it for aphrodisiacal purposes employed dogs to dig it.
22. (c) A special feature of the festival was the whipping of women on their stomachs and genitals.
23. (a) Some popular titles were *The Register of Girls*, *Stars of the Salons* and *Hints to Men about Town*. Some had a pocket at the back to hold condoms.
24. (d) Honest!
25. (b)
26. (b) Members of this strange club had to obtain a contribution from their own lady friends and in return they were allowed to kiss the wig.
27. (c)
28. (d)
29. (a) This was in 2590 B.C.
30. (c) The Romans believed that coitus would adversely affect their voices.
31. (d)
32. (d)
33. (a) The Topkapi's heyday was over by 1800, and it remained an effete relic until it became a mere monument after the revolution of 1909.
34. (c)
35. (b)
36. (d) Sappho committed suicide here.
37. (a) It started in the early 1900s.
38. (a) and (b) They were driven away by crowds of hostile spectators, however.
39. (c)
40. (d)
41. (c)

42. (b)
43. (a)
44. (a)
45. (b)
46. (c) They stretch upwards upto the level of navel and thus present the appearance of an inverted-V.
47. (a)
48. (a) They are so called because they were first described by a London surgeon William Cowper (b. 1666)
49. (c) Stroking the inside of thighs can stimulate these muscles reflexly and this elevation of testes can actually be seen.
50. (d)
51. (b)
52. (d) known so because of its shape.
53. (c)
54. (a)
55. (b)
56. (b) Reported by Neugebauer in 1886.
57. (c)
58. (d)
59. (a)
60. (c)
61. (b)
62. (a) Also called the 'mount of Venus' or the 'mound of love'.
63. (b)
64. (a)
65. (d)
66. (d) It is also called the maidenhead.
67. (b) During pregnancy, pigmentation may develop around the navel as well, which is known as *Areola umbilicus*.
68. (c) Each gland is a little larger than a pea. They were first described by the Copenhagen anatomist Caspar Bartholin (b. 1655).
69. (a)

70. (d)
71. (b)
72. (d) 200 million per day is also the rate at which testicles manufacture the spermatozoa.
73. (a)
74. (d) NPT stands for nocturnal penile tumescence. It indicates that the sleeper is dreaming.
75. (b) Most men under 50 spend 25% of their total sleep time in a state of NPT. After 50, this figure gradually falls to 15%.
76. (b)
77. (a)
78. (c) She experiences about 12 periods less for each child. A woman having 3 children would experience about 400 periods.
79. (d)
80. (b)
81. (a) However, after the ovulation has occurred, the temperature rises sharply and is maintained at a level about 0.8°F above that seen during the first half of the cycle.
82. (c) This was in 1863.
83. (d)
84. (c)
85. (d) Their semen is however devoid of spermatozoa.
86. (a)
87. (F) This is a widely prevalent myth.
88. (T) Ova are released during the middle of menstrual cycle.
89. (F) Some youngsters may be surprised at this answer. But the stunted or slow growth (if any) is not due to masturbation but due to their worrying about it.
90. (F)
91. (F) In fact, most men fail to have even a satisfactory sexual intercourse during the first night due to anxiety and lack of technique.
92. (F)
93. (T)

94. (T)
95. (F)
96. (F)
97. (T)
98. (F)
99. (F) Not necessarily. It merely denotes that your child is growing up healthily.
100. (T)
101. (F) In fact all children should be told about it.
102. (F)
103. (F) This operation can be reversed in many cases.
104. (F) In fact if you don't have a desire to masturbate, you are abnormal.
105. (F)
106. (T) This is very likely.
107. (T) Till date, this is a true statement.
108. (F) Hymen may rupture due to many other reasons.
109. (F) Old persons, as old as 90 years or more, have produced babies.
110. (F) The erect penis size is almost same for all men. Also it depends more on technique than on actual penis size.
111. (F)
112. (T)
113. (T)
114. (T)
115. (F) Not necessarily. Sometimes the hymen may be so flexible that it doesn't rupture on intercourse and thus no bleeding occurs. In fact some prostitutes have been known to have intact hymen, and they are known to surrender their "maidenheads" several times a night at premium prices.
116. (F) It is just messy, that's all.
117. (T) For best results, it must be rinsed by a spermicidal jelly or cream.
118. (F) People only think so because the horn resembles an erect phallus.

119. (F) They are all there — about 400,000 of them — in the two ovaries, at the time of birth. They are simply released after puberty in monthly cycles.

120. (F) Modern studies have demonstrated that male infants have erections and female infants manifest vaginal secretions. Sigmund Freud thought that the key zones of sexuality change with age. For instance in very young infants the key zone of sexuality may be the mouth.

121. (F) Less than one in four transvestites are gay.

122. (T) Older men frequently have ejaculations without achieving an erection.

123. (F) Watch her nipples. They became erect during orgasm.

124. (b)

125. (a)

126. (c)

127. (a)

128. (b) He was a French surgeon.

129. (c) It was the *nom de plume* of Eugene Schoenfeld, M.D., medical columnist of the San Francisco paper, *The Berkeley Barb.*

130. (d) Brown-Séquard (1817-94) was no quack. He described the results of hemisection of the spinal cord, still known as Brown-Séquard syndrome.

131. (a)

132. (c) Dr Kothari is currently Professor of Sexual Medicine at the Seth G.S. Medical College, Bombay, the only department of its kind in South East Asia.

133. (d)

134. (b)

135. (d)

136. (b)

137. (a) Lakshmi's other name.

138. (b)

139. (d)

140. (b)

141. (a)

142. (d) By this gesture he makes his word more sacred. This custom later became widespread throughout the ancient Near East.
143. (b) She is also known as Mylitta.
144. (a)
145. (c)
146. (b)
147. (a)
148. (d) The donkey is considered to be the embodiment of lust.
149. (b)
150. (c)
151. (a) The English word 'echo' comes from her story.
152. (a)
153. (b)
154. (d)
155. (c) Terpsichore is the Muse of the Dance.
156. (b) Many lapis lazuli amulets carved with her sacred symbol have been excavated.
157. (a) Platenoid 655 is named after her.
158. (b)
159. (d)
160. (b)
161. (c)
162. (a)
163. (d) Gary Cooper, who acted against her came to be known as the It Boy for his involvement with Clara.
164. (b) The offer was made in 1987. Graf refused.
165. (c)
166. (b) She also had 6 toes and 6 fingers.
167. (d) Poppaea (died AD 65) was the wife of the Roman emperor Nero.
168. (c)
169. (b)
170. (a)
171. (b) Asteroid no. 836 is called Jole.

172. (d) Her eighth marriage was solemnized in October 1991, with a construction worker Larry Fortensky.
173. (c) All the others were her husbands once only!
174. (a) Mike Todd died in an air crash on March 22, 1958, when he was going to New York in a private plane to receive an Oscar for his film *Around the World in 80 Days*. Liz couldn't accompany him because she had a bad cold.
175. (b) He was heir to the famous Hilton Hotel chain.
176. (d) Otero (1868-1965) was a Spanish courtesan. She was a strikingly beautiful woman, 5 feet 10 inches tall with measurements of 38-21-36. In her prime, she charged $ 10,000 a night for her services.
177. (c) Jean Harlow (1911-1937), well known for her films like *Hell's Angels* and *Bombshell*, also rubbed her nipples with ice to make them stand out for the camera, and dyed her pubic hair platinum to match the hair on her head.
178. (a)
179. (d) Lady Caroline Lamb (1785-1828), a British novelist, married him in 1805.
180. (a) After handing the magazine, Sharon (b. 1951) lifted her sweater up to her chin and struck the same pose. Yes, you guessed it right, the cheque was immediately cashed.
181. (a) Consequently, Lee (1914-70) defined the recipe for a good striptease as "more tease than strip"!
182. (c) Just before she committed suicide in 1962, she arranged for the magazine publication of some nude photographs of herself. It was at that time that she uttered this famous sentence.
183. (b)
184. (a) His lover was Hero, a priestess of Aphrodite.
185. (c)
186. (b)
187. (d)
188. (a)
189. (c)
190. (b)

191. (a)
192. (d)
193. (c) He even impregnated her, Danaë giving birth to Perseus sometime later.
194. (a) He impregnated her also, Leda giving birth to Helen and Polydeuces.
195. (b)
196. (d)
197. (c)
198. (a)
199. (b)
200. (a)
201. (d)
202. (c) Written by Thomas Hardy in 1891. She finally murders her rapist Alec, and is hanged as a murderess.
203. (a)
204. (d)
205. (d)
206. (b)
207. (a) It is because Othello wrongly accuses his wife Desdemona of infidelity.
208. (b)
209. (c)
210. (d)
211. (a)
212. (d)
213. (a)
214. (b)
215. (c)
216. (d)
217. (b)
218. (c)
219. (a)
220. (b)
221. (b)

222. (c)

223. (a)

224. (d)

225. (a) Later Proteus falls in love with Silvia and forgets Julia.

226. (c) Thurio is stupid but wealthy.

227. (a)

228. (d)

229. (c) Héloise and Abélard (1079-1142) are a fascinating and tragic couple, inseparably linked in the galaxy of lovers.

230. (a) Boulanger (1837-91), a French general shot himself two and a half months later to fulfil his promise.

231. (d) Later the suit was settled out of court.

232. (b)

233. (c) Queen Amytis had forsaken green and wooded hills of her native Media for the flat plains of Euphrates, when she married king Nebuchadnezzar. To make amends, he built her hanging gardens of Babylon.

234. (a) He married Theodora (500-547), notorious for her cruelty and lasciviousness.

235. (b)

236. (b)

237. (a)

238. (c)

239. (d) Surprisingly dyspareunia is quite common among women. In fact it is one of the commonest symptoms for which women seek gynaecological help.

240. (c)

241. (a)

242. (a) Section 12 (1) (a) of the Hindu Marriage Act 1955 provides for nullity of marriage on grounds of impotence only.

243. (d) Decrees of nullity of marriage have been passed by the judges on grounds of relative impotence.

244. (c) During frequent sexual activity, bacteria gain an entry into the bladder, a disease still known as *honeymoon cystitis*.

245. (b)

246. (c) In cases of imperforate hymen, the blood will collect in the vagina leading to haematocolpos.

247. (d)

248. (a)

249. (d)

250. (b)

251. (c) Phimosis makes erection extremely painful and coitus impossible, but it can be surgically corrected.

252. (a) François de la Peyronie (b. 1678), a Paris surgeon, first described this disease.

253. (d) Uxoravalents on the other hand can score with every woman except their wives.

254. (b) Greek goddess of love and beauty is Aphrodite from which the word "aphrodisiac" is derived.

255. (b)

256. (a)

257. (c) and (d)

258. (c) Spanish fly is actually a beetle, known also as blister-beetle, because when rubbed on skin it produces blisters. In India it is known as *Teleni Makkhi*, and occurs abundantly in rainy season in certain parts of north India and Kashmir.

259. (b)

260. (d) The girls were 27-year-old Betty Margaret Grant and 19-year-old June Florence Malins. In the court, Ford admitted that he had had sexual intercourse earlier with Betty about three months ago. The girls died because Spanish fly is a poison and is wrongly considered to be an aphrodisiac.

261. (b)

262. (d) This is a myth, however, which arose from an experiment done on rats in 1960s and 1970s. Rats deprived of Vitamin E developed certain sexual disorders which got treated when Vitamin E was administered.

263. (c) Galen (fl. 2nd century), was a Greek known as the prince of physicians; Ovid (43 B.C. — A.D. c17) was a Roman poet whose work mainly consists of erotic and mythological poetry; Sheikh Nefzawi was an Arab physician who wrote the book *The Perfumed Garden*, a book on herbs. They all considered honey as a great aphrodisiac.

264. (a) An ancient French proverb warns: "Those who wish to lead virtuous lives should abstain from truffles." Truffles are an expensive underground fungi with an exquisite flavour.

265. (b)

266. (a) Casanova, one of the busiest lovers in history, took 50 oysters at breakfast.

267. (d) Perhaps the belief in peaches' aphrodisiac powers arose because of its deep fur-edged cleft which resembled female genitalia. A sexually appealing girl is sometimes a 'peach' and peach house was once a common English slang for a brothel.

268. (c)

269. (b) Amyl nitrite can be dangerous to persons suffering from heart disease or abnormal blood pressure. A similar product, Butyl nitrate, which does not require a prescription, is used in the same way as Amyl nitrite.

270. (c) It is a substance generated in the bowels of whales and is usually found floating on the ocean.

271. (a) The manufacture of Absinthe with real oil of wormwood (*Artemisia absinthium*) is illegal in most civilized countries.

272. (c)

273. (a)

274. (b)

275. (d)

276. (c)

277. (a) Its common name Licorice is a corruption of the generic term *Glycyrrhiza*.

278. (b)

279. (c) Its toxic substances can numb the nerves of the arms and legs.

280. (b) Despite its popular designation, it is not a Ginseng at all.

281. (d) According to him, it was power!

282. (b)

283. (a)

284. (b)

285. (a) He was the French President who died on 16 February 1899, while engaged in a sex act with a high class French courtesan, Marguerite Steinheil.

286. (d)

287. (a) Briand (1862-1932), a Frenchman, won the Nobel Peace Prize in 1926.

288. (c) She asked for a like gift and Byron complied.

289. (b) This affair was hotly denied by the Eisenhower family. Kay was his staff driver.

290. (a) A photocopy of this letter still exists.

291. (d)

292. (c)

293. (b) Flynn died of a heart attack in Vancouver in 1959.

294. (d) To this his queen Caroline of Ansbach is reputed to have said, 'Ah, that need not hinder you.'

295. (d) He said it about Joséphine, his first wife.

296. (a) He died of an 'uncommon effusion of blood'. Some say the excitement was too much for him, others maintain that he was slain by another of his jealous wives.

297. (d) Leo VIII was Pope from A.D. 963-964 and succeeded by Benedict V.

298. (a) He is also reported to have been devoted to the *men* he loved.

299. (d) This incident has an interesting rejoinder. When the overseer told it to Calvin Coolidge, he asked, 'Same hen every time?' The overseer replied, 'oh, no, a different one each time.' Immediately the President said, 'Tell that to Mrs. Coolidge.'

300. (c)
301. (d)
302. (a)
303. (b) He drove his other two sisters into misery.
304. (c) Schönkopf, an innkeeper's daughter was his first love.
305. (c) The Romanians actually viewed Carol as a Casanova.
306. (a)
307. (d)
308. (b)
309. (c)
310. (a)
311. (d) Otero (1868-1965) was a famous courtesan, catering to such great people as King Leopold II of Belgium, Prince Nicholas I of Montenegro, Prince Albert of Monaco and Albert, Prince of Wales. This incident occurred in 1902.
312. (b) Sidonie Gabrielle Colette (1873-1954) was one of the most celebrated of French authors, having written 73 books in her lifetime.
313. (d)
314. (d)
315. (b) She was the wife of Emperor Claudius.
316. (a) Actually she wanted to say 'happiness'. Since the French can't quite pronounce the letter 'h', she said 'appiness. Her faulty pronunciation did the rest!
317. (b)
318. (c)
319. (a) The Vatican Library has a collection of 25,000 books on sex. Kinsey Institute, more properly known as The Institute for Sex Research, comes second with 20,000 books. The British Museum also has about 20,000 books.
320. (d)
321. (b) A woman aged 21 in Salonica was given an artificial vagina because of her deformity. The donor was her mother, aged 50.

322. (c) It was in October 1971.

323. (b) It was started sometime in 1987 by a husband and wife team — Dr Aniruddha and Anjali Malpani.

324. (c) Mae West records in her biography that once a man called Ted made love to her for fifteen hours!

325. (d) In the strictest sense a geisha is a 'singing girl', but there is nothing to prevent her from indulging in fornication. A geiko is a singing girl. A hokan is a male prostitute.

326. (a)

327. (c) An okasan buys a maiko from her parents as a child, to evade the law against slavery.

328. (d) Haori means 'coats'. These girls refuse to sell their bodies.

329. (b)

330. (a)

331. (b) In *mixoscopia bestialis*, the individual observes intercourse between a person and an animal to reach a sexual climax.

332. (a)

333. (c)

334. (b)

335. (d)

336. (a)

337. (c) The word Lesbian comes from the name of this island.

338. (b)

339. (c)

340. (a) Para means deviance and philia means attraction.

341. (d)

342. (a)

343. (c)

344. (b)

345. (a) Such people are known as voyeurists.

346. (b)

347. (a)

348. (c)

349. (d) This is usually done in a tightly packed bus.

350. (b)

351. (a) The arousal can be by things like sweaty underwear or used menstrual pads.

352. (c)

353. (b)

354. (a)

355. (d)

356. (c) Because they have a popular appeal, we find many nymphomaniacs in novels and movies, yet they are extremely rare in real life.

357. (b) Also known as transvestism. The term eonism is derived from the name of a Frenchman Chevalier d'Eon de Beaumont (1728-1810) who practised this perversion.

358. (a)

359. (c) In fact right through the Middle Ages, Ganymede typified homosexuality. The Latin version of his name is the derivation of the word 'catamite' which refers to the passive male partner among homosexuals.

360. (d) The leading lesbian of her time, Natalie (1876-1972) was also a writer of epigrams, memoirs and poetry.

361. (a) Strictly speaking troilism is sexual activity between three partners; either two males and a female or two females and a male. In the cited example, the husband is the third partner, who acts mainly as a voyeur.

362. (b)

363. (b)

364. (a) The term is derived from the classical myth in which Clytemnestra, wife of Agamemnon, fell in love with her husband's cousin, then killed Agamemnon.

365. (c)

366. (a)

367. (d) Strictly speaking, the term refers to derivation of sexual pleasure from conversing with a member of the opposite sex in obscene language. It is considered a symptom of psychic impotence.

368. (b)

369. (c)
370. (b) Supposedly named after Dippold, a German schoolmaster.
371. (d) This is a French term and from this derive the slang expressions ""gam" and "gamming". Traditionally the practice is known as cunnilingus.
372. (c) Air enters the uterus, from where it is carried by veins to the lungs. In the tiny vessels of lungs, the air acts as a seal, thus stopping circulation. This is known as air embolism.
373. (b) To achieve this, a noose is wound round the neck at the time of masturbation. A slight carelessness may lead to accidental hanging. FBI estimates that 500-1000 unintentional deaths occur every year in this fiendish way.
374. (c)
375. (a)
376. (d)
377. (b)
378. (c)
379. (d) Silk and velvet are common fabrics of this class.
380. (c) The term is Latin for 'the erotic horse'.
381. (d)
382. (a)
383. (c)
384. (b)
385. (b)
386. (c) Ben-wa balls are made up of plastic, steel or even gold. They come in sets of two or more, all of which are hollow except one which is filled with mercury. They are inserted in the vagina.
387. (d)
388. (d)
389. (a)
390. (b)
391. (d)
392. (c)
393. (a)

394. (d)
395. (a)
396. (a)
397. (c) At the time of marriage, a woman is legally deemed to have given voluntary consent to sexual intercourse throughout her life, so (b) is not a correct answer.
398. (c)
399. (d)
400. (c)
401. (b)
402. (a)
403. (d)
404. (c)
405. (a)
406. (b)
407. (d)
408. (c)
409. (b)
410. (c)
411. (a)
412. (b)
413. (d)
414. (d)
415. (a) The first issue is now so much in demand that collectors pay as much as $ 400 for it.
416. (b) The exact figure in 53,991.
417. (a)
418. (b) Art Paul also worked as the art director of *Playboy*.
419. (b)
420. (d)
421. (b)
422. (d)
423. (c)
424. (a)
425. (b)
426. (b)

427. (a)
428. (a)
429. (b)
430. (c) and (d) Both of them are contemporary American psychologists and sex researchers and studied at the University of Minnesota.
431. (d) He was a Massachusetts doctor.
432. (b)
433. (c)
434. (a) and (b)
435. (b) and (d)
436. (b) and (d)
437. (a)
438. (b)
439. (d) He was of the Vatsyayana family. Commonly people know him only as Vatsyayana.
440. (d)
441. (b) Burton translated it in the 1880s.
442. (d) It was written by a Dutch gynaecologist Van de Velde.
443. (a) In 1968, Picasso created 347 erotic engravings most of which were printed in this issue of *Avant-Garde.*
444. (c) Anthony Comstock (1844-1915) acted as a self-appointed crusader against immorality in literature.
445. (a) It also gives 8 forms of love-scratch.
446. (d) In Arabic it means 'Pleasures of Women'.
447. (d)
448. (b)
449. (c)
450. (a)
451. (c)
452. (d)
453. (c)
454. (b)
455. (b) It was in the April 1970 issue of *Penthouse.*

456. (a)

457. (d)

458. (b)

459. (c) Henriques is a Jamaican social anthropologist.

460. (a) The title translates as *Secret Codes of the Jade Room.* An example: A woman must have big and thick labia, if she has a big mouth and thick lips!

461. (b)

462. (d)

463. (a) Its editor is Al Goldstein. The magazine has featured such articles as 'Ten Famous Pussies and How They Taste'!

464. (b) Sellon (1820-68), who was actually an eccentric, shot his brains out in a London hotel.

465. (c)

466. (a) Such a kiss is common among Hawaiians, Tongans, Eskimos and Malays.

467. (b) They were frequently burnt at stake.

468. (c) and (d)

469. (c) They are prized as a feminine erotic attraction among certain tribes. Girls without this apron are considered unfit for marriage.

470. (d)

471. (a)

472. (a) and (b)

473. (c)

474. (b) This is a strange custom prevalent in many world communities. In Hindus for instance a younger sister can't marry if the elder sister remains unmarried for some reason. In such cases the elder sister marries a tree and clears the way for the younger sister.

475. (a) The custom is known as the temporary transfer of conjugal rights.

476. (d)

477. (d) According to ancient Roman law, no virgin — be she a citizen, slave, pagan, or Christian — could be executed.

478. (d)

479. (b)
480. (a). The father even shows some symptoms of pregnancy and labour pains. The symptom is perhaps a sympathetic reaction.
481. (c) This custom is prevalent among the Kikuyus of Kenya who permit girls to visit their male friends in a special hut where they eat and sleep together, without sexual intercourse.
482. (a) Also spelt as Lata or Lattah. It comes from a Malay word meaning ticklish.
483. (d)
484. (b)
485. (d) By this act he becomes her son, for it is considered that he has sucked at her breast.
486. (c) We find figures of a breast and an egg after the signatures of Cleopatra, but no such figures appear in the signatures of Ptolemy.
487. (a)
488. (c)
489. (b)
490. (d) It was usually done by inserting a metal ring in the prepuce in the males and through the labia in females.
491. (a)
492. (c) Streaking started as a fashion in 1974.
493. (d)
494. (a)
495. (c) However the girl's legs were tied to prevent the obvious! The system was prevalent in Scottish Highlands till 19th century.
496. (d) The Greek historian Herodotus (fl. 5th Century B.C.), considered this the wisest of Babylonian customs.
497. (a) He married his sister Isis.
498. (d) The object of this strange custom was to rupture the hymen and neutralize the superstitious fear of defloration.
499. (c) Sometimes the widow was even married to her deceased husband's heir. The purpose was to protect

the widow economically and socially. This custom was most common among the ancient Hebrews.

500. (d)

501. (c) As in the case of the Pandavas.

502. (d)

503. (b)

504. (a) The converse is exogamy which is marriage outside one's group.

505. (c)

506. (a)

507. (b)

508. (d) This was prescribed by the medieval Catholic church.

509. (c) Also known as *jus primae noctis*. It has been said that it was one of the causes of the French Revolution.

510. (d) Quite similar to *jus primae noctis* of Europe. It was an occasion of pride rather than for shame for the girl's parents, who paid costly gifts to the priest to do this duty. Poor girls had to wait for years before their turn came and they couldn't legally marry till they had had intercourse with the priest.

511. (a)

512. (d)

513. (c)

514. (a)

515. (d) However, within a fortnight, he confessed his sexual relations with Keeler, because a London newspaper had a copy of a compromising letter he had sent Keeler. He then had to resign.

516. (a) He was an osteopath, who actually introduced Keeler to Profumo.

517. (c) After this incident Hugo returned to his original mistress Juliette Drouet.

518. (a) By June 1787, Burns had become successful and sure enough Mr Armour changed his opinion about him. Once he even locked his daughter with Burns in her bedroom to ensure a happy reunion.

519. (c) Adverse publicity from this scandal even affected Steffi's game, costing her a few championships.

520. (b)

521. (c) After the lapse of a few days, the girl returned to her chagrined parents. Today people still gather here to hear the latest gossip, generally political.

522. (b) When this slander came to Adam's ears, he said, 'If this is true, General Pinckney has kept them all for himself and cheated me out of my two.'

523. (d)

524. (d) Daisy sold her exposé to Bernard MacFadden's *New York Evening Graphic.* Daisy was found guilty of embezzlement and jailed for a year, but the scandal damaged Clara's career.

525. (a) Despite her charges, US senate confirmed Judge Thomas by a vote of 52 for and 48 against.

526. (b)

527. (a) The charge couldn't be proved, but it ended Arbuckle's career as a comic. He died alone and forgotten on June 28, 1933.

528. (a)

529. (c)

530. (d) They committed many more sex murders, and their trial in 1965-66, widely known as the Moors murders trial, led to agitation for the restoration of the death penalty.

531. (b) John Reginald Halliday Christie was hanged at Pentonville on 15 July 1953, for the murders which he committed during the long span from 1943 till 1949.

532. (a) Cummins murdered and mutilated four women in London in February 1942. He was hanged on 25 June 1942.

533. (d) Fish, a 66-year-old father of six, cooked the flesh of his female victims and ate it with vegetables which kept him in a state of continuous sexual fervour.

534. (b) Over 46,000 sets of fingerprints were taken in this remarkable case. Set no. 46253 matched Griffiths'. He was hanged at Walton Prison on 19 November 1948.

535. (c) Nelson raped and strangled twenty women before he was hanged on 13 January 1928 at Winnipeg.

536. (d) Heirens was judged insane and sentenced to three consecutive life terms.
537. (a) He committed ten murders with rape and raped another twenty women. He was sentenced to a total of 140 years in prison.
538. (c) Rees, a 28-year old professional musician, was executed in 1961.
539. (b) He reduced Boston to near-panic in the early 1960s.
540. (a)
541. (c)
542. (d)
543. (b)
544. (d)
545. (a) The male runs away in terror.
546. (c)
547. (d) In addition to these three, testes are intra abdominal also in amphibians, reptiles and birds.
548. (d)
549. (a)
550. (b)
551. (d)
552. (b)
553. (a)
554. (b)
555. (b)
556. (c) 12 days. For the others: (a) 14 days; (b) 14 days; (d) 15 days
557. (a) The Alpine Salamander takes up to 38 months to give birth at altitudes over 1400 metres in the Swiss Alps, though this drops to about 25 months at lower altitudes
558. (b)
559. (a)
560. (d) He was referring to a strange anomaly in the German language whereby the German word for girl (Mädchen) has a neuter gender but turnip (Rübe) has a feminine gender.

561. (c)
562. (a)
563. (c) She was the wife of last Viceroy of India.
564. (d) She made this reply when a reporter asked her how she went about writing her memoirs.
565. (a) She said this when she learnt that a life jacket had been named after her.
566. (b) In fact it has been suggested that all Picasso's work is in some sense erotic.
567. (d)
568. (c)
569. (b) Mae West (1892-1980) is the creator of the largest number of witticisms regarding sex. Her other memorable remarks are "I've been in more laps than a napkin", "I used to be Snow White, but I drifted", "He who hesitates is a damned fool", "Whenever I'm caught between two evils, I take the one I've never tried", and "She's the kind of girl who climbed the ladder of success wrong by wrong".
570. (a) Henry Miller (b.1891) was an American author.
571. (b)
572. (d)
573. (c)
574. (a)
575. (a) Evelyn Waugh (1903-66), British novelist was mainly a social satirist.
576. (b)
577. (d)
578. (a)
579. (c)
580. (a)
581. (b) He made this remark in the film *All You've Ever Wanted to Know about Sex.*
582. (a)
583. (b) Cary Grant (b. 1904), a U.S. actor born in Britain, said this at the age of 72.
584. (d)
585. (a)

586. (c)
587. (a)
588. (b)
589. (a)
590. (c)
591. (a)
592. (d)
593. (a)
594. (c)
595. (d)
596. (b)
597. (a)
598. (c)
599. (a)
600. (d)
601. (c)
602. (a)
603. (d) On 12 July 1987 she said again, 'I said ten years ago that in ten years time it would be smart to be a virgin. Now everyone is back to virgins again'.
604. (c)
605. (b)
606. (a)
607. (d)
608. (d)
609. (c)
610. (a)
611. (b) Freud made several interesting remarks about sex. Two famous ones are 'No marriage is secure until the wife had succeeded in making herself a mother', and 'the sexual life of a civilized man is seriously disabled'.
612: (a) La Belle Otero was the professional name of Augustina Otero Iglesias (1868-1965), the illiterate daughter of a town prostitute in Spain. She grew up fatherless and in poverty.
613. (b) William Gladstone made the initial taunt.

614. (a) Eisenhower (1890-1969), 34th president of the United States married Mamie Geneva Doud in 1916.

615. (c)

616. (a) Pope Alexander VI (c.1431-1503), born as Rodrigo Borgia was notorious for his immorality and extravagance.

617. (c) Sophie Arnould (1740-1802) was a popular French actress.

618. (d) During the previous day, at a buffet luncheon, when Churchill politely asked his hostess for a second helping of chicken breast, she had remarked, 'Mr. Churchill, in this country we ask for white meat or dark meat.'

619. (a) He was the son of the famous Alexandre Dumas Pére.

620. (d) Ninon de Lenclos (1620-1705), was a French courtesan whose fans included such figures as the playwright Molière and the philosopher Saint-Evremond

621. (d) Pope John XXIII (1881-1963) was Pope from 1958 to 1963.

622. (a) Nancy sweetly retorted, 'Winston, you are not handsome enough to have worries of that kind.'

623. (d) Philip Roth's book in question was *Portnoy's Complaint,* which was competing in the bestseller lists with Susann's *The Love Machine* at that time.

624. (a)

625. (b)

626. (a) Dorothy Parker (1893-1967) is known for her sexy puns.

627. (d) Zsa Zsa Gabor (b. 1919), Hungarian-born US movie and television star was noted for her sexiness and her numerous marriages. Once when asked how many husbands she had had, she looked puzzled and asked rhetorically, 'You mean apart from my own'?

628. (b)

629. (c) Robert Charles Benchley (1889-1945) was an American humorist.

630. (a)

631. (d) Joséphine (1769-1821) was Napoleon's wife and very unfaithful.
632. (a) She had failed to get a child from him.
633. (d)
634. (a)
635. (d)
636. (a) Nadeau was the editor of *Les Lettres Nouvelles*
637. (d) Douglas was a justice of the US Supreme Court.
638. (a)
639. (d) Gypsy Rose Lee is the stage name of Rose Louise Hovick (1914-70), American striptease performer. She made this comment just before her death from cancer.
640. (c)
641. (d) Girodias (b. 1919) was a French publisher of literary books with an explicit sex content.
642. (a) Sophie (1740-1802), French actress and opera singer, said it about a rival actress who consistently produced a child every year. With her sagging figure she lost both theatrical engagements as well as her lovers.
643. (d) Henri (1822-97) was a French aristocrat, son of king Louis Philippe.
644. (a)
645. (d) de Valera (1882-1975), thrice prime minister of Ireland, said it after a visit to France.
646. (c)
647. (d)
648. (a)
649. (d) Luhan, an American heiress and writer was a lover of D.H. Lawrence and gave him a hundred-and-sixty-six acre ranch in New Mexico.
650. (b)
651. (a) The statue is now known as the *Borghese Venus.* Pauline was the sister of the great Napoleon.
652. (c)
653. (d)
654. (d)
655. (b)

656. (a)

657. (c) He went on to say, 'On this point all my sympathies are with the nudists.'

658. (d)

659. (b)

660. (a)

661. (d)

662. (c) Miss Lawrenson is an American journalist.

663. (b)

664. (c) Wrate, editor of the nudist magazine *Sun and Health,* said it in response to a male novice's fear that he will disgrace himself by getting an erection.

665. (a) Julia (39 B.C. - A.D. 14) was Agrippa's wife, who was chief minister in her father's (Augustus's) cabinet.

666. (d)

667. (b).

668. (a) It is also known as the 'Curse of Venus'.

669. (c)

670. (b) It is actually a misnomer. The discharge that occurs in gonorrhoea is pus, not semen, as believed earlier.

671. (a) In many of Shakespeare's plays syphilis is referred to simply as 'the pox'. In advanced syphilis the skin breaks out in many pocks, which do not heal easily (especially true in Shakespeare's days when penicillin was not discovered)

672. (d) It was brought back possibly from Haiti by Columbus's sailors.

673. (c)

674. (b) NGU stands for Nongonococcal Urethritis.

675. (a)

676. (c)

677. (c) The bacillus was discovered by the Italian dermatologist Augosto Ducrey (1860-1940), after whom it is named. Its biological name is *Haemophilus ducreyi.*

678. (a), (b) and (d)

679. (a) and (b) In 1983 Prof. Luc Montaignier of the Institute Pasteur in Paris and Robert Gallo of the National Cancer Institute, isolated the virus independently.

680. (d)

681. (c)

682. (d) Of these 2,043 people were in Maharashtra, 1,429 in Tamil Nadu and 1,347 in Manipur.

683. (c)

684. (d) Dr Kien of the New York University Medical Centre was one of the first physicians to diagnose the disease.

685. (a)

686. (b) They live mainly as passive homosexual agents.

687. (d)

688. (c)

689. (a)

690. (b) He was changed into a beautiful female, April Ashley, who in 1963 married one Mr. Corbett.

691. (d) The operation was done in 1952 on one George Jorgensen who was changed to Christine. He phoned his parents saying, "I am now your daughter."

692. (a)

693. (b)

694. (d)

695. (c)

696. (c) Other slang terms for female pubic hair are beard, broom, brush, feather, nether eyelashes, shaving brush and tail feathers.

697. (b) Dreadnought in normal English refers to a type of heavily armed battleship.

698. (d)

699. (b)

700. (c)

701. (a) Other slang expressions for being pregnant are 'have a lump in front', 'have a dumpling on', 'have a nine-month dropsy' and 'have one's cargo aboard'.

702. (c)

703. (d)

704. (a) From the image of the vulva.

705. (b) Other slang terms to deflower a woman are 'cop a cherry', 'crack a pitcher', 'pick her cherry' and 'trim the buff'.

706. (c) Other slang terms for human testes are apples, Beecham's pills, bullets, cannon balls and family jewels.

707. (c)

708. (d)

709. (b) Also known as catamites.

710. (d)

711. (a)

712. (c) This is purely for reasons of appearance.

713. (a) Italian word *diletto* means delight.

714. (c)

715. (b)

716. (a)

717. (c)

718. either (a) or (b)

719. (d) The term is sometimes used by homosexuals as a slang term for penis.

720. (a)

721. (b)

722. (c)

723. (a)

724. (d)

725. (b)

726. (c)

727. (d) This film earned three and a half million dollars.

728. (b) Naseeruddin Shah couldn't give dates, so Aparna Sen hired a most unusual person for the lead role — her own husband. Mukul Sharma has been the editor of *Science Today*, from 1985 till Feb. 1992.

729. (a) In this 1941 production Jane Wyman and Regis Toomey kiss for a record period of 3 min. and 5

sec. This single kiss accounted for 4% of the film's total running time!

730. (d)

731. (c)

732. (a)

733. (b)

734. (c)

735. (a) The mermaid would be obliged to live with the man who seized her comb and would even bear his children, but the moment she got her comb back, she would return to the sea, never to be seen by her husband and children.

736. (d)

737. (c)

738. (b) He was a Danish sculptor.

739. (d) The term is Satyriasis.

740. (b)

741. (c)

742. (a)

743. (b)

744. (d)

745. (b)

746. (a) Roman emperor Tiberius was said to be one of her patrons.

747. All. In addition, he had two more wives; Catherine Howard and Catherine Parr.

748. (b)

749. (d) Valeria Messalina (d. A.D. 48) is reputed to have made love to twenty-five men at the same time, and to have forced noble Roman ladies to prostitute themselves as low-class debauchers in front of their husbands.

750. (b) He also christened his crew 'Flynn's Flying Fuckers'.

751. (a) The team was called 'The Thundering Herd'. The legend grew that Clara took on more than a single player at a time.

752. (c) Sir Francis (1708-81) was an English rake and amateur Satanist.

753. (b) Lily Langtry (1852-1929) later became the mistress of Prince of Wales.

754. (d) Milnes (1809-85) was one of the few M.P.s who vigorously attacked the first Obscene Publications Act (1857), though he did not disclose his personal interest in the matter.

755. (a)

756. (c)

757. (b)

758. (d) In A.D. 66, a rival courtier turned Nero against him and he was forced to commit suicide.

759. (a) This incident combined with his general manner earned him the reputation of a sadist.

760. (c)

761. (a)

762. (b)

763. (d) The erotica still remain in locked cases.

764. (b)

765. (a)

766. (d)

767. (c)

768. (a) "To Bowdlerize" now means prudish expurgation.

769. (d)

770. (b) Robert Burns (1759-1796) was Scotland's national poet.

771. (a) Now only 5 percent of her total output remains.

772. (d)

773. (a)

744. (d)

775. (c) This book hit the top ten in 1980.

776. (a) Jean Genet (b. 1910) lived for a while as a thief and pimp. This epic was written in pencil on brown prison paper, during his imprisonment.

777. (b) Olympia was the first publisher to publish such books as *Lolita, Candy* and *The Ginger Man.*

778. (a) Procopius (A.D. 499-565) first worked as a lawyer. Antonina was Belisarius's wife, who openly conducted a passionate affair with her adopted son.

779. (c) Once her friend asked her where she got her beautiful pearls? "Never mind," replied Mae West, "but you can take it from me that goodness had nothing to do with it." This riposte became so famous and well-known that she later used it as the title of her autobiography.

780. (a) Balzac even exclaimed once, "This morning I lost a novel."

781. (d) The unexpurgated text was finally passed for publication in 1960, after a lengthy trial involving numerous expert witnesses. It is one of the rare books in the whole history of publishing to go on trial for obscenity.

782. (c) It was written by Vladimir Nabokov, a Russia-born American.

783. (b) It is said of Elsett-Budur in Arabian Nights.

784. (d) It continued until A.D. 1695.

785. (a)

786. (c)

787. (b)

788. (d) The theory failed to find any takers however.

789. (a) The work was called *Monsieur Nicolas.*

790. (c)

791. (b)

792. (a)

793. (c)

794. (b)

795. (d)

796. (a)

797. (c)

798. (a)

799. (b)

800. (d)

801. (c)

802. (a) *Howl* had a strong homosexual content, and included the then taboo word fuck.

803. (b)

804. (a)

805. (d)

806. (c)

807. (d) Binet (1744-1800) is also known for his 124 illustrations for Restif's *Contemporaines.*

808. (a) and (b) They are contemporary American psychologists and sex researchers.

809. (c) and (d)

810. (a)

811. (b) PPP stands for Progressive Political Pornography group. These cartoon strips contain many overtly sexual scenes. For instance in one scene, the horn of a dead bull is shown sticking up between Octobriana's legs.

812. (d) Léopold Robert (1794-1835), Swiss painter and etcher, killed himself out of unrequited love.

813. (c) Honest!

814. (a)

815. (d)

816. (b)

817. (b)

818. (b)

819. (c)

820. (a)

821. (d) It is named after a nearby street.

822. (c) Perennius's (*ca.* 50 B.C. - A.D. 10) works were first found in 1882.

823. (b)

824. (a)

825. (d)

826. (b) Fellini (b.1920) starred his wife Guilietta Masina in some of his pictures. *Satyricon* is an orgiastic picture showing bestiality, sodomy, tribadism and bondage.

827. (b)

828. (a)

829. (d)

830. (b) Steinheil (1869-1954) was also the central figure in the scandal of the president's death, which led to an attempted *coup d'etat* shortly afterwards.

831. (a)

832. (a)

833. (c)

834. (b)

835. (d)

836. (a)

837. (c)

838. (a) It was widely rumored that Servilia had also prostituted her daughter, Tertia, to him.

839. (d) Temple prostitutes are different from ordinary prostitutes in the sense that they have got religious sanction. They generally belong to scheduled castes and tribes.

840. (c)

841. (a) Parasurama was Yellamma's son.

842. (b)

843. (a) She was nicknamed "Our Lady of the Orient" and "Madame la Générale".

844. (d)

845. (d) Koriyo people mostly live in Chingleput near Madras

846. (b) Theodora (500-547) later became empress of Byzantium.

847. (a) This was in China in 650 B.C., when the Chinese statesman Kuang Chung licensed prostitutes for the first time in history.

848. (c) Having the same name as the goddess she admired.

849. (d) This was in A.D. 89.

850. (a) This was in A.D. 1158.

851. (c) In A.D. 1220.

852. (b)

853. (a) Not only that, she showed her contempt by baking the note in a pie and eating it for breakfast.

854. (d) Cora Pearl (1835-1886) was also described as the last word in luxury.

855. (c) Lais, a Corinthian, fled to Thessaly secretly, escaping from her many lovers. The women of that country being envious and jealous of her beauty dragged her to a shrine of Aphrodite and stoned her to death.

856. (d)

857. (a)

858. (b)

859. (d) These were the mistresses of wealthy patrons.

860. (b) He had only seven wives.

861. (a) He had seven hundred wives.

862. (c) He had an additional eighteen wives.

863. (a)

864. (d)

865. (b)

866. (c)

867. (a)

868. (d)

869. (b)

870. (c) They were usually drunk on *blitum,* a cheap wine.

871. (b)

872. (c)

873. (a)

874. (b)

875. (d)

876. (c)

877. (b)

878. (a)

879. (c)

880. (d)

881. (a)

882. (b) Platenoid 409 is named Aspasia.

883. (d) The monarch eventually conceived such an admiration for the thief's ingenuity that he gave him the same daughter in marriage.

884. (a) and (b)

885. (c)

886. (a)

887. (b)

888. (d) Ned Ward describes this club in detail in his *Secret History of Clubs* (1709).

889. (c)

890. (a)

891. (b)

892. (b) *Fenneli* literally means fennel, a type of exotic herb much used in pickles.

893. (a) When Mrs. Berkely died in 1836 after a highly successful career, the horse was exhibited at the Royal Society of Arts in Adelphi, London.

894. (c) It has been said that if the face of Helen of Troy (c. 1200 B.C.) was capable of launching 1,000 ships, then a unit of beauty sufficient to launch one ship should be called a millihelen.

895. (a)

896. (b) She won it in 1966. She was a medical student.

897. (a)

898. (d) It was staged at Atlanta City, New Jersey.

899. (a) Surprisingly she had only a 30″ bust.

900. (d)

901. (b) It was inaugurated in Long Beach, California.

902. (c)

903. (b)

904. (a) This is the reverse of Oedipus complex.

905. (c) This is the reverse of Electra complex.

906. (d)

907. (c)

908. (a)

909. (b)

910. (b)

911. (a) Greek "orchis" means testicle which the bulbous double roots of the plant resemble. In medicine, the term "orchitis" means inflammation of the testicle.

912. (b)
913. (d)
914. (a)
915. (b)
916. (c)
917. (b)
918. (c) In French it is called *Le Vagin,* meaning it has a masculine gender!
919. (c)
920. (a) They are like "Hijras" in India.
921. (b) It was because Muslims abhor women exhibiting themselves in public.
922. (d) Because when inflated, it resembled a well-developed bust.
923. (a)
924. (c)
925. (d) It showed erotic art, films, sex aids, striptease, etc; and by all accounts was an immense success.
926. (a) It is a port in Denmark.
927. (a)
928. (b) It was known as Comstock Law and forbade distribution of even contraceptive information.
929. (d) Comstock especially objected to Shaw's play *Mrs. Warren's Profession* on grounds of obscenity and in revenge Shaw coined this term.
930. (c) It is claimed that the penis was obtained by Napoleon's confessor-priest. It was listed as "a small dried-up object".
931. (b)
932. (d) Not surprising in the precontraceptive era!
933. (a) Nine months and two weeks after the incident Augusta gave birth to a daughter, Medora.
934. (c) It is because Onan in Bible was the first man supposed to have masturbated.
935. (b) This method was common in nineteenth century France and then known as *la chamade* ("the retreat"), *la prudence* and *la discrétion.* Other names for this method are *coitus abruptus,* and *coitus incompletus.*

936. (d) The female partner in this case kneels in a knee-chest position.

937. (c) Coitus comes from Latin *coire* meaning to come together.

938. (a) This method is also known as *Coitus Saxonius.*

939. (d) Other names for this method are Male continence and Oneidà method. In 1847 John H. Noyes established the Oneida Community, first in Vermont and a little later in New York. This community used *coitus reservatus* for the first time.

940. (b) Latin word *manus* means hand and *stupratio* means defilement. That's why a synonym of masturbation is manustupration.

941. (c) Bekker was a minister with minimum medical knowledge. His account was more a religious condemnation rather than a medical one. He will go down in history as the perpetrator of one of the most dreadful myths regarding human sexuality. This book appeared in 1716.

942. (b) Bankhead (1903-68) was famous for her flamboyant life style — "more of an act than an actress," as an anonymous wit said.

943. (c) Lady Godiva persistently pleaded with her husband King Leofric to reduce taxes on people. To silence her, Leofric made this outrageous suggestion. Seventeen-year-old Godiva did this act in 1057.

944. (d) In the *Book of the Dead,* Isis is shown kneeling before him, her mouth around his sacred phallus.

945. (a)

946. (b)

947. (a)

948. (d)

949. (c) Very few cases of this strange phenomenon have been recorded. An excellent review appeared in *British Medical Journal* of 20 Oct. 1979.

950. (d) The legend perhaps reflects a deep fear of rape among these tribes. An excellent review appeared in *British Journal of Medical Psychology* (1943).

951. (a) No actual case has been recorded, but folk stories among many tribes give a graphic description of it.

952. (c) In 1875, Marcel de Leclure, a Parisian painter wrote a love letter to his girl friend, containing the phrase *je vous aime* (I love you) 1,875,000 times. He had to hire a secretary to do the letter for him.

953. (d)

954. (a)

955. (d) Derived from the Latin *gaude mihi* — 'give me pleasure'.

956. (b)

957. (a) This French word means "buttock position".

958. (c) The term originally referred largely to homosexual behaviour, but it also applies to heterosexuals.

959. (a) The exact meaning of the term is "primary position for sexual intercourse".

960. (d) Greek *gymnos* means "being nude". In early Greece, nudity was common in many public places such as gymnasia.

961. (c) The position is prevalent in the islands of the Pacific.

962. (b)

963. (a)

964. (c)

965. (d) Dimples are supposed to be the imprints of angels' kisses and remain main invitations for men to kiss. Two dimples are also seen in a woman's back, and this fact has been exploited by sculptors of the nude.

966. (c) In Greek 'phryne' means toad.

967. (b) In the seventeenth and eighteenth centuries Italy, gifted male singers were castrated before puberty to preserve their contralto and soprano voices.

968. (d) A boy infatuated with his mother frequently imagines that the jealous father would castrate him.

969. (a) It was the major instrument of censorship in Catholic Europe. In short it is simply known as *The Index.*

970. (a) It was issued by the Council of Trent.

971. (d) This was exploited by both English and French publishers for the production of erotica.

972. (c) These wigs of pubic hair were made for ladies who had lost their own through smallpox!

973. (a)

974. (b) Greek *porne* means harlot and *graphy* means writing.

975. (b) He was struck blind for his folly.

976. (d)

977. (a)

978. (c) It was held at Taj Palace Hotel. Keynote speakers were Dr. Kothari, Vasant Sathe and Mulk Raj Anand.

979. (b) They also began calling a nudist colony as Sun Club.

980. (a) His daughter was Julia, who was banished to Pandateria off the Campanian coast, where she remained till her death.

981. (b)

982. (d)

983. (b) It also undertakes sex education by means of lectures and seminars at schools and universities.

984. In this picture the Egyptian goddess of sky, Nut is shown arching above the god of Earth, Geb. Geb impregnates Nut with the stars. This drawing is based on the Papyrus of Tameniu (21st dynasty) at the British Museum. This representation is so common in Egyptian drawings that some scholars think that Egyptians preferred a female-on-top position during sexual intercourse.

985. He is Dr Alfred Charles Kinsey (1894-1956), American biologist, sexologist and pioneer statistician of sexual behaviour, who interviewed about 20,000 people on matters of sex and published what is now widely known as 'The Kinsey Report'.

986. This is a toothed urethral ring, which was used during the nineteenth century to treat nocturnal emissions. It was worn over the penis and when during an erotic dream, the penis enlarged, the teeth would 'bite' into it, thus awakening the patient.

987. This is a variant of the contraption encountered in the last question. It was also used during 19th century.

988. This looks like a scientific instrument, but actually it was a device used in nineteenth century to prevent night emissions. It was worn over the penis and any tumescence of penis would complete the circuit and cause a bell to ring awakening the person.

989. This is a chastity belt which soldiers in middle ages used whenever they went out for long wars. They made their wives wear it, locked it and took away the key with them. Erotic genital organs of the female were guarded by a toothed opening which precluded any chance of her cuckolding her husband. Specimens of this belt can be seen in museums all over the world, especially the Cluny Museum in Paris.

990. The artist is Aubrey Beardsley, an English painter who lived in nineteenth century. He died of tuberculosis at the age of 25.

991. This is called 'Locking Pockets'. Its patent no. was 995,600 and it was granted on June 20,1911. Invented by one J.E. Heyser, the invention provided for a sheet metal plate fitted with metal pockets for the reception of the penis and testicles. The contraption was supposed to prevent any attempt on the part of the wearer to masturbate.

992. He is Giovanni Giacomo Casanova (1725-1798), an Italian adventurer who is reputed to have seduced thousands of women of almost all nationalities. He is the most famous womanizer of all time.

993. She is Mae West (1892-1980), U.S. movie star and actress and the sex symbol of the 1930s. Her best known films were *She Done Him Wrong* (1933), *Klondyke Annie* (1936) and *My Little Chickadee* (1939).

994. She is Briggitte Bardot, the daughter of a Parisian industrialist. She became known as 'BB' and caused much sensation because of her defiant shamelessness.

995. She is Raquel Welch, who has been called the Sixties' answer to Monroe.

996. She is Marlene Dietrich (b. 1904), German actress and singer, who electrified the silver screen with her cool, sophisticated sexuality in the 1930s and 1940s.

997. She is Jane Russell who was handpicked for fame by billionaire Howard Hughes. She was one of the sexiest ladies of her times.

998. She is Pamella Bordes, who shot into fame in 1989, because of her alleged sexual relations with respectable members of British Parliament.

999. This is *osculum infame* or the kiss of shame. In the medieval times, during the feast day of Sabbat witches assembled together and kissed the buttocks of the Devil who took the form of a billy goat. This act of profane obeisance marked the witches' profession of faith to Satan.

1000. He is Dr. Prakash Kothari, noted sexologist of India and writer of the book, *Orgasm: New Dimensions.*

1001.

a. Amharic
b. Arabic
c. Cambodian
d. Chinese
e. Danish
f. Dutch
g. Farsi
h. Finnish
i. French
j. Gaelic
k. German
l. Greek
m. Hausa
n. Hebrew
o. Hopi
p. Hungarian
q. Indonesian
r. Italian
s. Japanese
t. Korean
u. Lao
v. Lingala

w. Mohawk
x. Navaho
y. Norwegian
z. Polish
aa. Rumanian
bb. Russian
cc. Sioux
dd. Spanish
ee. Swahili
ff. Swedish
gg. Thai
hh. Turkish
ii. Vietnamese
jj. Welsh
kk. Zuñi